Managing Desktop Publishing

How to Manage Files, Styles, and People for Maximum Productivity

Jesse Berst

New Riders Publishing
Thousand Oaks, California

Managing Desktop Publishing

How to Manage Files, Styles, and People for Maximum Productivity

Jesse Berst

Published by:

New Riders Publishing
PO Box 4846-V
Thousand Oaks, CA 91360
U.S.A.

All rights reserved. No part of this book may be reproduced or transmitted in any form or by any means, electronic or mechanical, including photocopying, recording, or by any information storage and retrieval system without written permission from the authors, except for the inclusion of brief quotations in a review.

Copyright ©1989 by New Riders Publishing

First Edition 1989

Printed in the United States of America

Library of Congress Cataloging-in-Publication Data

```
Berst, Jesse.
  Managing Desktop Publishing.

  Bibliography: p.
  1. Desktop publishing--Management.   I. Title.
Z286.D47B47   1989      686.2'2068        89-3242
ISBN 0-934035-27-X
```

Warning and Disclaimer

This book is designed to provide information about desktop-publishing procedures. Every effort has been made to make it as complete and as accurate as possible.

However, no warranty of suitability, purpose or fitness is made or implied. The authors and New Riders Publishing shall have neither liability nor responsibility to any person or entity with respect to loss or damages in connection with or arising from the information contained in this book.

Trademarks

Many of the designations used by manufacturers and sellers to distinguish their products are claimed as trademarks. Where these designations appear in the book and the authors were aware of a trademark claim, the designations have been printed with initial capital letters.

Apple, LaserWriter and Macintosh are trademarks of Apple Computer, Inc.
AutoCAD is a registered trademark of Autodesk, Inc.
Hewlett-Packard and LaserJet are trademarks of Hewlett-Packard Co.
IBM, IBM PC, IBM PC AT, and IBM PC XT are trademarks of International Business Machines Corporation.
Microsoft Word and MS-DOS are registered trademarks of Microsoft Corp.
Multimate is a registered trademark of Ashton-Tate.
ODMS is a trademark of Odesta Corporation.
PostScript is a registered trademark of Adobe Systems, Inc.
Unix is a trademark of AT&T Bell Laboratories.
VAX is a trademark of Digital Equipment Corp.
Ventura Publisher is a registered trademark of Ventura Software, Inc.
WordPerfect is a registered trademark of WordPerfect Corporation.
WordStar is a registered trademark of MicroPro International Corporation.
Xerox and Xerox Writer are registered trademarks of Xerox Corp.

Acknowledgments

Although one name appears as author, this book is really a compilation of ideas developed by a group of DTP devotees. Thanks to Rusty Gesner, Pat Haessly, Carolyn Porter, Lisa Kirk, Jon DeKeles, Harbert Rice, Jim Cavuoto, Bob Moody, Byron Canfield, Chad Canty, Barbara Roll, Keith Thompson, and Ellen Brout for sharing their suggestions and techniques. Special appreciation goes to Martha Lubow, who prepared the first draft of several chapters.

The ideas and tips on writing in Chapters Six and Seven were gathered over the years from many generous authors and editors, some of whom I have met in person and others only on paper. They are too numerous to mention individually, but I thank them for their willingness to share the tricks of their trade.

Production

Lead Editor: Barbara Roll

Cover design: Jill Casty

Page design: Martha Lubow, Barbara Roll

Illustration: Keith Thompson

About the author

Jesse Berst has authored or co-authored eight computer books, including the bestsellers *Inside Xerox Ventura Publisher* and *Publishing Power with Ventura*. He has written hundreds of articles about desktop publishing and related topics for magazines such as *PC World, Small Press, Personal Publishing, Business Software* and many others. He has been a featured speaker at national computer, business, and publishing conventions.

An honors graduate of the University of Puget Sound with a degree in business, he is currently Director of the Electronic Publishing Division of New Riders Publishing, an independently-operated subsidiary of Que Corporation.

Contents

Introduction
How this book can help　　　　　　　　　　　　　　　i
How this book is organized　　　　　　　　　　　　　ii
Who can use this book　　　　　　　　　　　　　　　iii

Part One — How-To

Chapter 1, Supervising Desktop Publishing
Why your job is harder now　　　　　　　　　　　　1-1
Organizing for efficiency　　　　　　　　　　　　　1-3
Building your own tool kit　　　　　　　　　　　　1-13

Chapter 2, Creating Text
File handling tips　　　　　　　　　　　　　　　　2-1
Typing guidelines　　　　　　　　　　　　　　　　2-13
Preformatting text files　　　　　　　　　　　　　2-25
An author's tool kit　　　　　　　　　　　　　　　2-33

Chapter 3, Creating Pictures
Why and when to create pictures　　　　　　　　　　3-2
How to create pictures　　　　　　　　　　　　　　3-3
Naming picture files　　　　　　　　　　　　　　　3-13
Marking and describing pictures in the text　　　　3-18
An illustrator's tool kit　　　　　　　　　　　　　3-24

Chapter 4, Editing
The mechanics of editing　　　　　　　　　　　　　4-2
Copyediting　　　　　　　　　　　　　　　　　　　4-6
Proofreading　　　　　　　　　　　　　　　　　　4-15
Indexing　　　　　　　　　　　　　　　　　　　　4-20
An editor's tool kit　　　　　　　　　　　　　　　4-24

Chapter 5, Formatting pages
    Organizing the project   5-2
    File conversion and cleanup   5-3
    Page layout   5-5
    Job tracking   5-14
    Archiving   5-16
    A formatting tool kit   5-17

Part Two — Reference

Chapter 6, Sample Grammar and Usage Guide
    Building a usage guide   6-2
    Usage Rules   6-3

Chapter 7, Sample Writing Guide
    New Riders' Writing Guide   7-2
    Improving the organization   7-3
    Improving the mechanics   7-17
    Improving the style   7-28
    Continuing on   7-33

Chapter 8, Tag Dictionary
    The New Riders tag system   8-1
    Body Text and variations   8-5
    Captions   8-9
    Callouts   8-10
    Headings and Titles   8-11
    Lists   8-16
    Notes   8-22
    Other   8-24
    Tables   8-25

Chapter 9, Sample Checklists
    Book production   9-2
    Magazine production   9-6

Chapter 10, Bibliography and Resources
    Books   10-1
    Magazines & Newsletters   10-4
    Associations   10-5

Appendix A
    Installing the Optional Disk   A-1

Introduction

Take one personal computer. Add word-processing and page-layout software to taste. Stir in a group of novice operators and place in a 72-degree office for one month. What do you get?

Confusion. Consternation. Chaos.

To bake a cake, you need more than ingredients. You also need a recipe and implements. To run a desktop-publishing (DTP) operation, you need more than hardware and software. You need a plan, and the tools to put that plan to work.

This book will help you create a DTP strategy and a DTP *tool kit* tailored to your way of working.

How this book can help

Managing Desktop Publishing will help you get more out of your current system. If you're just getting started, it will help you get up and running as easily as possible.

It's smart to learn from your mistakes — but it's even smarter to learn from the mistakes of others. This book shares solutions discovered by veteran users (the hard way, in many cases). Many of these solutions are common sense. Others are traditional techniques adapted to desktop publishing. Still others are new technologies. By using the right mix of these ingredients, any desktop publisher can come up with the recipe for success.

You *can* have your cake and eat it too. You can have the power of desktop publishing without reinventing the methods to manage it. By learning from the experiences of DTP pioneers, you can build an efficient, cost-effective publishing operation with a minimum of time and effort.

How this book is organized

This book has two main sections. Part One is the how-to portion, which outlines specific techniques in detail.

Chapter One, "Supervising Desktop Publishing," helps you devise an overall strategy. It explains the five aspects of desktop publishing, and what you need to successfully bring them together.

Chapter Two, "Creating Text," explains how to get a manuscript ready for desktop publishing. It proposes a simple file-naming system, clarifies typing guidelines, and shows you how to benefit from the power of preformatting.

Chapter Three, "Creating Pictures," delves into the illustration process. It offers solutions to the troublesome problems of naming and locating pictures, marking them in the manuscript, and captioning them.

Chapter Four, "Editing," explains how to integrate editing into the DTP workflow. It includes time-saving tips on copyediting, proofreading, indexing, and more.

Chapter Five, "Formatting Pages," shows you how to easily and efficiently merge text, pictures, and editing into a final document.

Part Two is a reference section. Its five chapters provide full-scale, real-life examples of the tools and techniques explained in Part One, along with additional resources. You can use the example chapters as the starting point for your own tool kit. (All of the example documents are included on the optional Managing disk, for those who want to get started as fast as possible.)

Who can use this book

Managing Desktop Publishing has ideas for anyone who produces pages with a personal computer. Its practical, down-to-earth techniques apply whether you have a Macintosh, a PC, or a Unix workstation. *Managing* also applies whether or not you are part of a team. Workgroup publishers will appreciate the methods for integrating members' contributions. But those who work on their own can also benefit. Organization and efficiency are as important to a single user as they are to a workgroup.

So you don't need any particular brand of hardware and software to use *Managing Desktop Publishing*. Nor do you have to be part of a large corporation. All you need is an interest in efficiency — doing more work with less effort.

The first step to efficient desktop publishing is understanding the big picture. And that's precisely the focus of Chapter One, "Supervising Desktop Publishing."

How-To

Part One

Supervising Desktop Publishing

1

This chapter will help you gain control of your desktop-publishing (DTP) operation. Its three sections provide an overview and suggest ways to manage DTP:

- why your job is harder now
- organizing for efficiency
- building your own tool kit

Let's start by examining DTP's impact on a company. In many cases, DTP makes a manager's job *harder* than before.

Why your job is harder now

You brought desktop publishing into your company because it promised advantages:

- time savings
- cost savings
- better-looking documents

DTP does indeed bring benefits. But it can also create problems:

- confusion about what to do (and when to do it)
- conflicts about overlapping responsibilities
- lack of standards and controls

Because of these problems, desktop publishing can conceivably take more time and money while giving you uglier documents. Consider, for instance, the Washington State research institute that brought in Macintosh computers and DTP. Eight months later it studied the results. Management was shocked to find out that desktop publishing had made things worse.

True, DTP had eliminated outside typesetting bills for the institute. But the cost of documents was higher than before. The institute's engineers and researchers were enamored with the new toys. They spent their expensive time fiddling with formats and trying out new tricks. In some cases, they spent more effort on a document's *look* than on its *content*.

Moreover, each user was coming up with unique designs. None of the bids, proposals, and reports looked like any of the others. And the appearance of these documents was distinctly worse than the old versions. Meanwhile, the graphic arts department was underutilized, even though its personnel had the skills, interest, and training to use DTP effectively.

Today, the firm has a well-defined desktop-publishing strategy. Its researchers spend their time researching, not designing documents. Designated people in each department are responsible for converting raw material (in the form of text and picture files) into finished documents that match company standards. Today, DTP makes an important contribution to the firm's profits and competitive position.

Along the way to this happy ending, the company had to invent methods and controls like the ones explained in this book. They could have reached the promised land months earlier. How? By installing a plan for supervising DTP at the same time they installed the hardware and software.

The manager's role

So now we come to the crux of the problem. DTP requires all the controls of traditional publishing *and then some*. Before desktop publishing, you were probably responsible for one portion of the total production. Perhaps you wrote the text. Then you handed it off to someone else — an editor, or a typesetter, or an illustrator, or whoever. The point is, from then on it was their baby.

Now you've got to raise the baby on your own. You are expected to handle an entire project from start to finish. DTP makes it possible to accomplish any and every part of prepress production from a single desktop. But here's the other side of the coin: DTP makes it possible to *foul up* any part of the process from a single desktop.

Desktop publishing forces people into new roles. Traditional job descriptions go out the window when any person can accomplish any task from his desk. Unfortunately, traditional controls often disappear too. Without these checks and balances, nobody knows who's responsible for what.

It's up to the manager to sort things out again — to decide *who's* going to do *what* and *when* they should do it. The purpose of this book is to help you with that job. Here's our central premise: To profit from DTP you must do two things: 1) organize for efficiency, and 2) give everybody on the team the tools they need to do their part of the job.

Organizing for efficiency

DTP organization usually falls prey to the *burglar-alarm syndrome*. Nationally, 80 percent of all burglar alarms are installed *after* a robbery has taken place. Likewise, most efforts at DTP organization occur *after* things become so chaotic that productivity suffers.

Common sense says that it's smarter to install an alarm before you get robbed. Likewise, it's smarter to organize before work bogs down. True, it does take some up-front effort to establish an organizational scheme. It also requires discipline to stick with it, especially at first. Soon, however, people come to prefer the organized system because it's easier, simpler, and faster than haphazard methods.

We recommend that you look at ways to organize your office, your people, and your projects right away, whether you've already encountered problems or not.

Organizing the office

Now that you're involved in desktop publishing, you're going to have more files to handle — more paper files, and more electronic files. You'll soon be swamped unless you build a system in advance.

Your job is even harder if you work on several projects at a time, or if you have multiple versions of a single document. It is easy to misplace the marketing report you finished last week; or to copy the old version of a layout file on top of the new one; or to forget which picture files are which.

We're not going to waste much time explaining how to set up paper files. We'll content ourselves with repeating the motto of an NFL football team: Just do it. And do it *in advance*.

You don't need a graduate degree to figure out a logical, efficient filing system. For instance, you can give each project a separate folder. Store everything for that project in that folder — printouts, pictures, disk backups, everything. Complex projects will require further subdivision, but the same principle applies. For instance, you could create a separate file for each chapter of a long book; or each issue of a monthly newsletter; or each client project for your desktop-publishing service bureau. If you have multiple projects going at the same time, assign different colors to each one.

Organizing electronic files can also be simple and straightforward. All you need is 1) a standard method of naming files and 2) a standard way of organizing those files on your disks. Chapter Two, "Creating Text," explains naming and organization for text files. Chapter Three, "Creating Pictures," does the same for picture files. We'll save the details for those chapters. For now, suffice it to say you should build a system before you start dumping multiple documents onto the hard disk.

Organizing the people

In many ways, the organization of people is closely related to the organization of projects (as discussed later in the chapter). When we say organizing the *people*, we mean dividing responsibility on a broad scale. When we say organizing the *project*, we're referring to the small-scale task of divvying up the work for a particular undertaking.

You can't just give people DTP tools and expect them to produce good-looking documents. You have to provide the necessary knowledge and training. Then you have to keep users in contact with one another so they have a source of solutions.

One of the first problems is deciding who should work with desktop publishing. Not everyone is suited the job. Desktop publishing takes a mix of skills. People with production experience may not know computers. People with computer skills may not have design know-how. In general, however, it's easier for a skilled publisher to learn the computer than it is for a computer technician to learn publishing skills.

You must also consider personal preferences. Some people may not want a new job on top of their old ones — especially if it comes as a surprise. For instance, a Midwest textbook publisher ran into resistance when it installed desktop publishing on editors' desks. The editors were afraid of the new technology. They also felt they had enough to do without adding page layout. The solution was to hire and train a DTP specialist for each editorial department.

Ironically, it can work the other way, too. Some people are overeager to work with desktop publishing, at the expense of their regular duties. Conflicts can arise if you fail to make it clear who has the authority to make decisions. When a well-known Santa Monica think tank brought in desktop publishing, a year-long battle ensued. The department heads insisted on the authority to use DTP as they saw fit. The production department countered that it should have the responsibility.

A solution that has worked for the think tank — and for many other companies — was to designate a desktop-publishing leader. This person develops procedures and sets standards. One San Francisco software house, for instance, has a "DTP czar." She created the initial procedures and document designs, then trained one person in each department. Those people then trained the others to use the same procedures and standards.

Training is a second, seemingly obvious solution. However, it often goes overlooked until trouble arises. DTP is too complex to absorb in a few days. People need time away from their regular work loads. Or, you can phase in desktop publishing in stages. Begin by performing one task with DTP, the rest traditionally. Then add another phase. Eventually, the entire operation will move smoothly to DTP.

Training must be ongoing. One East Coast entertainment corporation, for instance, has regular user-group meetings to share problems and solutions. Once again, this company has provided each department with a DTP expert. The user-group meetings give the in-house experts a place to get further help.

Perhaps the most important part of assigning responsibility is to decide who will set the standards. Many companies fail to establish document guidelines in advance. As a result, DTP can end up detracting from the company image.

For example, a Minnesota manufacturing company brought in DTP and failed to set any standards. The organization's designers went wild with the new tools. They were broadcasting the look of ten companies, instead of one — ten trendy, cutting-edge companies. But that wasn't the impression management wanted to give. Now the firm has given design responsibility to a single person. The resulting documents conform to the solid, conservative image management has decided is best for sales.

If we do not change our direction we are likely to end up where we are headed.

Organizing the project

Once you've made some broad-brush decisions about organizing the office and the people, you are ready to tackle individual projects. Successful project management has two key aspects: 1) dividing the work and 2) monitoring the progress.

The first job is to dividing up the task. Before you can do that, you must understand the five phases of desktop publishing.

The five phases of DTP

This section won't be a long one because it doesn't need to be. Some books on desktop publishing contain long lists of tasks and responsibilities along with complex flow charts. It doesn't need to be that complicated. Although there are many individual components, desktop publishing breaks down into five basic parts:

1. Supervising — overseeing the entire process and making sure the other parts work together.
2. Creating text — writing the words (and preparing the file for DTP).
3. Creating pictures — producing the illustrations.
4. Editing — checking and improving the words and pictures.
5. Formatting the pages — merging the edited text and pictures into a final document.

Those of you with traditional graphic arts experience may wish to examine Table 1-1. It lists the five phases along with some of the job titles typically associated with each one.

It is much easier to suggest solutions when you know nothing about the problem.

Table 1-1. Traditional job titles for the five phases of desktop publishing.

Supervising	Publisher
	Executive editor
	Managing editor
	Project manager
	Lead editor
	Production manager
Text	Author
	Writer
	Contributing editor
	Columnist
	Contributor
Pictures	Illustrator
	Artist
	Photographer
Editing	Editor
	Copy editor
	Proofreader
	Technical editor
	Expert reader
Formatting	Designer
	Typesetter
	Paste-up artist
	Layout artist
	Graphic artist
	Production manager

Table 1-2 lays out the major tasks. In real life, things don't happen in neat categories or precise order. Jobs overlap, work proceeds in parallel, chores have to be redone. Nevertheless, if you are new to DTP, this list will help you understand the big picture. Chapters Five and Nine contain more detailed discussions of project planning and production checklists.

Table 1-2. Major tasks in a desktop-publishing project.

Supervising	Determine goal and scope of project.
	Define target audience.
	Set schedule.
	Determine budget.
	Assign responsibilities.
	Develop guidelines for all other phases.
	Monitor progress.
Text	Create outline.
	Write first draft.
	Write additional draft.
	Put text file into proper format.
Pictures	Create thumbnail sketches.
	Produce first draft artwork (drawings, charts, photos, etc.).
	Create final artwork.
Editing	Read text and suggest changes.
	Review pictures and suggest changes.
	Verify corrected text and pictures.
	Proofread.
Formatting	Design pages.
	Lay out pages.
	Proof camera-ready pages.

Monitoring progress

Once the tasks have been divided, you must still monitor progress. You'll find a wealth of computer tools available to help with planning, scheduling, and job tracking:

- word processors with document summary capabilities
- outliners
- hypertext
- project-management programs
- dedicated document managers

For instance, many word processors include a summary screen. You can use the comments line to mark production notes, and the version line to track the revision level (Figure 1-1).

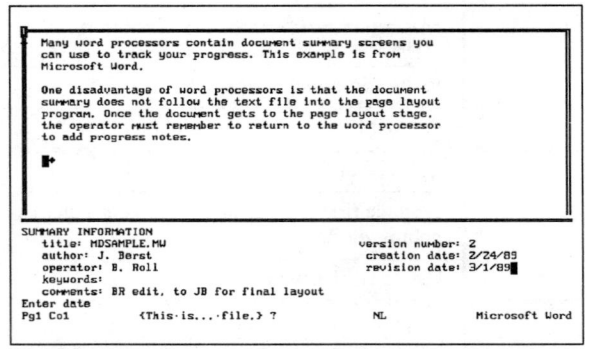

```
Many word processors contain document summary screens you
can use to track your progress. This example is from
Microsoft Word.

One disadvantage of word processors is that the document
summary does not follow the text file into the page layout
program. Once the document gets to the page layout stage,
the operator must remember to return to the word processor
to add progress notes.


SUMMARY INFORMATION
   title: MDSAMPLE.MW
   author: J. Berst                       version number: 2
   operator: B. Roll                      creation date: 2/24/89
   keywords:                              revision date: 3/1/89
   comments: BR edit, to JB for final layout
Enter date
Pg1 Col        {This is...·file.} ?          NL         Microsoft Word
```

1–1. Many word processors contain document summary screens you can use to track progress. This example is from Microsoft Word.

The real purpose of books is to trap the mind into doing its own thinking.

One disadvantage of word processors is that the document summary does not follow the text file into the page-layout program. Once the document gets to page-layout stage, the operator must remember to return to the word processor to add progress notes.

You can also buy dedicated document management software to work with some layout programs. For instance, the Odesta Document Management System (ODMS) is a family of software applications for workflow and document management (Figure 1-2). It runs on both Macintosh and VAX computers and is compatible with different page-layout and word-processing programs.

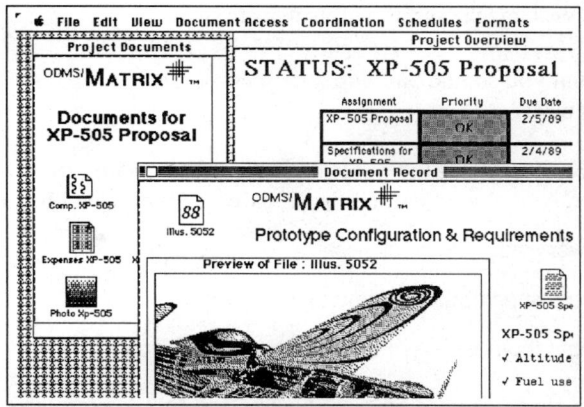

1–2. The Odesta Document Management System is a database that allows managers to track the location and progress of multiple documents.

Xerox Ventura Publisher users have access to Desktop Manager from New Riders. Desktop Manager is a utility program that runs inside Ventura to add dozens of new features, including job tracking, document summaries, management reports, and many more (Figure 1-3).

Chapter Five, "Formatting Pages," mentions a few ways to integrate job tracking into the page-layout function. Still, you shouldn't expect high technology to solve your planning woes. Computer software can be

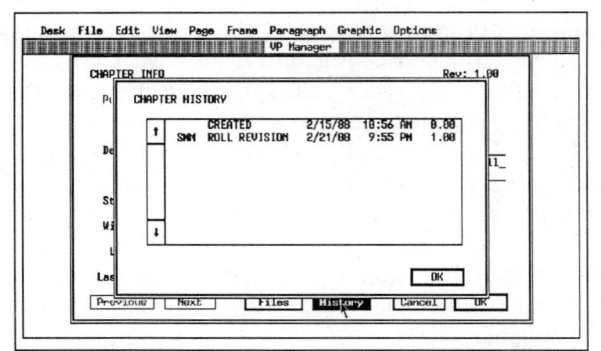

1–3. Desktop Manager from New Riders runs inside Xerox Ventura Publisher to add auxiliary features.

helpful, but you should build up to it. Incorporate it in stages as the need becomes clear.

Indeed, for many desktop publishers, the best planning tools are pencil and paper. As we've explained above, the essence of scheduling is simple:

- List every stage in the project.
- Assign responsibility to someone.
- Estimate the time it will take and assign a due date.

From there, you simply need to institute regular meetings or progress reports. Review Chapter Nine, "Sample Checklists," for a simple way of tracking due dates and responsibilities with checklists.

Building your own tool kit

Earlier we said that successful desktop publishing demands 1) organization and 2) tools for every member of the team. The remainder of this book is devoted to helping you assemble a tool kit of your own. This section gives you a preview and explains the supervisor's role.

You need more than lumber to build a house. You need a blueprint and you need tools. You need more than hardware and software to build a viable DTP operation. You need a blueprint (a plan). And you need tools.

In some cases, DTP tools involve computer technology. For instance, an editor's tool kit will probably contain an electronic spell checker, and perhaps a computerized grammar checker and thesaurus as well.

But in many cases you can create valuable aids with a pencil and a piece of paper. Since you have a desktop-publishing system, you probably won't be content with that — you'll want to dress them up. Still, the principle is a simple one: Once you've figured out how to do something, write it down. Then pass it around to all the people involved so they don't have to reinvent the wheel.

Chapters One through Five suggest tools for the various phases of a project. Let's take an advance look:

Author's tool kit

- File-naming system
- File-location guidelines
- Typing guidelines
- Tag list or formatting settings
- Tag dictionary
- Macros for preformatting
- Templates for preformatting
- Grammar and usage guide
- Writing guide
- Spelling and capitalization glossary

Illustrator's tool kit
- File-naming system
- File-location guidelines
- Formatting guidelines
- Text guidelines
- Standard frame (picture) sizes and/or picture templates

Editor's tool kit
- Writing guide
- Grammar and usage guide
- Spelling glossary
- Style list
- Copyediting and proofreading checklists
- List of proofreading marks
- File-naming and file-location guidelines
- Formatting guidelines
- Reference books
- Software

Formatting tool kit
- Conversion/cleanup checklist for word-processing files
- File-naming and file-location guidelines
- Formatting guidelines
- List of proofreading marks
- Tag lists and dictionaries

- Document templates
- Production checklists
- Job-tracking software
- Disk labels

You'll notice that we haven't included a separate tool kit for supervising DTP. That's because almost all of the tools we've mentioned are also valuable to the manager. For instance, the same production checklist that keeps the layout operator from forgetting key steps can help the manager monitor progress.

If you're responsible for overseeing desktop publishing, it will be up to you to assemble the tool kits for your office. Even if you delegate the actual work, stay involved in the decision-making. The tips and techniques suggested in this book represent more than a way to improve efficiency. They are also a method of circulating and enforcing standards.

However, before you can create customized tool kits for each person on your team, you need to decide just which tools should be in each one. To get started with that job, turn to the next chapter, which discusses creating text for desktop publishing.

Creating Text

2

This chapter is devoted to the mechanics of producing a text file. It contains suggestions that make it easier and faster to turn a raw manuscript into a finished document. It does not deal with grammar, usage, or style. Those aspects of writing are covered in Chapters Six and Seven.

We divided the chapter into three sections:

- file-handling tips
  how to name and organize files for efficiency and productivity
- typing guidelines
  how to keyboard text so the resulting file merges smoothly into the page-layout program
- preformatting techniques
  how to speed production by doing part of the formatting directly in the text file

File-handling tips

One of the quickest, easiest ways to improve your desktop-publishing operation is to streamline your file-handling procedures.

At first glance, file handling might seem trivial. You'll change your mind, however, the first time you format a 50-page chapter with the wrong text file and have to start over. Or put an incorrect technical drawing into the contract specifications. Or can't find a brochure you did six months ago and have to build it again from scratch.

File handling is, in fact, a stumbling block for almost all desktop publishers. Fortunately, it is an easy hurdle to overcome. The keys are 1) establishing a file-naming system and 2) setting standards on where to place those files.

How to divide material into files

Before we get into the details of a file-naming system, we should spend a moment on what to put into those files. We offer a few general suggestions below. Discuss these issues with your layout operator to determine whether exceptions will be needed.

The best strategy is to create a single text file for each logical unit. If you produce books, create one file for each chapter. If you produce newsletters or magazines, put each article into a separate file. Let the layout operator handle the chore of integrating the separate pieces into a unified whole.

Here are a few things *not* to do, based on real- life horror stories:

- Don't put an entire book into one file.
- Don't put an entire newsletter or magazine issue into one file.
- Don't arbitrarily divide chapters or articles into separate files.
- Don't put tables into separate files. Type them right into the text file at the spot where they should appear.

Setting up a naming system

A standardized naming system is the first secret of better file handling. In this section, we'll explain a system powerful enough for workgroup publishing, yet simple enough for everyday use by small departments.

If you currently use a Macintosh or Unix system, you may think you are immune from file-naming problems. Although DOS permits only 11 letters, the Macintosh allows up to 31, and Unix an almost unlimited number (Figure 2-1).

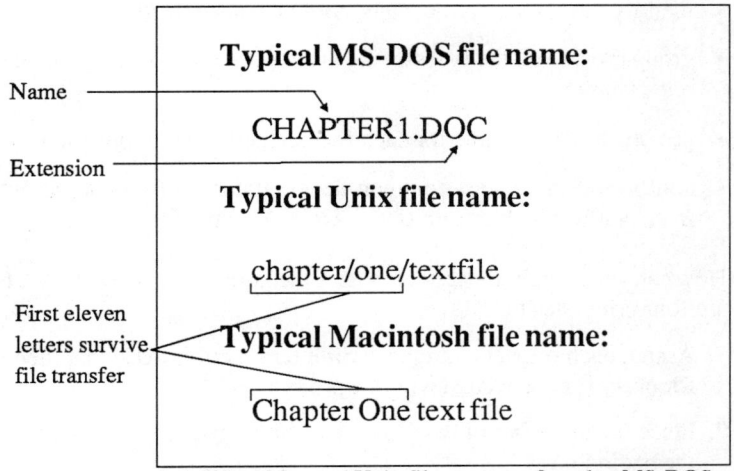

```
                    Typical MS-DOS file name:
    Name ─────────┐
                  ↘
                    CHAPTER1.DOC
    Extension ────────────────↗

                    Typical Unix file name:

                    chapter/one/textfile
    First eleven
    letters survive  Typical Macintosh file name:
    file transfer
                    Chapter One text file
```

2–1. When Mac and Unix files are transferred to MS-DOS, only the first eleven letters of the name are carried across. Plan your naming system so it can survive the transfer.

Despite their ability to use longer names, we recommend that Macintosh and Unix users stick to the short, PC-style names described below. Sooner or later, they will need to trade files with a colleague or service bureau using IBM PCs. When this occurs, only the first 11 letters of the file names will survive the transfer.

It's best, therefore, to use the PC approach right from the start. Keep in mind that code-based naming systems fall into the *hard-to-learn but easy-to-use* category. Although they may take more effort the first few times, they soon become faster and easier to use than longer names.

NOTE TO MACINTOSH USERS: If you want to use longer names, start the file name with the PC-compatible system explained below. Then put additional comments inside parentheses. Most translation routines strip out anything enclosed in parentheses when sending from the Macintosh to the PC.

Before we get into specifics, let's define what a naming system needs to accomplish:

- identify the subject, project, and format at a single glance
- group files, so all the files for one project can be moved or copied with one command
- provide a unique name for each file, so there is no duplication
- conform to the lowest common denominator, so files can be moved from platform to platform (DOS, Unix, Macintosh)

How can you achieve these goals within the limitations of MS-DOS? Here are four principles to follow:

1. Assign each project a unique, two-letter identifier. Use that identifier for *every* file associated with the project.
2. Place the identifier in the same place in every file name (probably at the beginning).
3. Use the rest of the file name to identify the specific file.
4. Use the extension (the three letters after the period) to identify the file format.

Now we'll use these principles to build a file-naming scheme for books. Then we'll explain how to apply the system to magazines, newsletters, and marketing materials.

A naming system for books

Assume that we are working on a book with 10 chapters. We'll use this book as an example. Here are a few typical text files from this project:
```
MD01.TXT
MD02.WS
MD03.DOC
```

Publishing: It's not just a job, it's... never mind, it's just a job.
Berst's advice to neophyte publishers

Setting up a naming system 2–5

Let's examine how and why we arrived at these names and what they tell us. The first two characters identify the project. The second two characters identify the chapter. The extension specifies the file type. (More about extensions later.) Consider, for instance, the file name MD01.TXT:

- MD = Managing Desktop Publishing
- 01 = First chapter
- .TXT = ASCII text format

Capital letters aren't necessary, but we find they make file names stand out. Notice that we include the zero before chapters one through nine, as in MD01, MD02, etc. (Be sure to use the character for zero, not a capital *O*.) This type of numbering makes it easier to sort and manipulate related files on the computer.

The two-letter code (MD, in this case) identifies the project and distinguishes it from all others. To make it easy to spot, we put this code at the beginning of the name. Even if the files for this project are mixed in with many others on a disk, they will all be listed together if we sort alphabetically. Likewise, we can move or copy all of them at once with global commands. For instance, here's an MS-DOS command that would copy all the files that start with MD:

COPY MD*.* A:

In a similar fashion, we could choose to copy only those files related to chapter one:

COPY MD01*.* A:

NOTE: If we had not inserted the zero in this file name, (MD01*.*), the copy command would copy MD1*.* and MD11*.* files.

MS-DOS allows up to eight letters in a name. We still have four left. We could have used them to say more about the file with names like these:
    MD01CHAP.TXT
    MD02CHAP.WS
    MD03CHAP.DOC

In our opinion, that's redundant, but there's nothing wrong with using the extra letters if it makes things easier for you. Some companies prefer to have all their file names exactly eight characters long.

Applying the system to other parts of the book

By now it's apparent how the system works for chapters. What about the other parts of a book — the appendices, indexes, and so on? One possibility is to give special sections their own two-letter code, to match the two-number code used to segregate chapters:

MD01.TXT (chapter one)
MDFR.TXT (front matter)
MDTC.TXT (table of contents)
MDAA.TXT (Appendix A)

As with the rest of the naming system, this suggestion won't work unless writers 1) have a summary sheet listing the approved abbreviations and 2) can be convinced to abide by it. Figure 2-2 summarizes the simple naming system for text files we use at New Riders.

Applying the system to other files

For a naming system to work, *all* files must follow the same pattern. Although this chapter is about text files, it is important to understand that the system extends to all other files as well.

Consider Xerox Ventura Publisher, a page-layout program, by way of example. Ventura uses the original text files to build documents. It also creates additional files — chapter files, caption files, style sheet files, and others. Notice how the naming system extends to the other files associated with the first chapter:

MD01.TXT (text file)
MD01.CHP (chapter file)
MD01.CAP (caption file)
MD01.VGR (Ventura graphics file)
MD.STY (style sheet)

You'll notice that the style sheet does not include a chapter identifier. We use the same style sheet for every chapter in a book. If you use a different

Project summary

Working title _____
Editor/phone _____
Final due date _____ Project code (2 letters) _____

Sample text file name

____ ____ • ____
(project code) (2 digit chap#) (file extension)

Chapter codes	Text file type	Extension
CV (cover copy)	ASCII	.TXT
FR (front matter)	DCA	.DCA
TC (table of contents)	MS Word	.DOC
00 (introduction)	Multimate	.MM
01 (Chapter One)	WordPerfect	.WP
02 (Chapter Two)	WordStar	.WS
etc.	Xerox Writer	.XWP
AA (Appendix A)	Xywrite	.XYW
AB (Appendix B)		
etc.		
DX (index)		
OR (ordering section)		

2–2. A summary sheet similar to this one will help you remember and apply a naming system.

one for each chapter, then it should be named accordingly: MD01.STY for the first chapter, MD02.STY for the second, and so forth.

Quark Xpress on the Macintosh does things differently from Ventura. It creates a single layout file for the entire document. Nevertheless, you can still adopt the system. Here's how you might name a chapter in Quark:
  MD01

As mentioned earlier, you should put additional comments (if any) inside parentheses so they won't transfer to the PC:
  MD01(first draft)

Quark optionally allows you to save the text to a separate file after layout. Here again, you can still use the system. To save the first chapter to a Microsoft Word text file:
    MD01.DOC

Text file extensions

So far we've seen how to construct a text file name that designates both project and chapter. We recommend that you use the extension (the three letters that follow the period) to show the file format. Most page-layout programs can accept text files from a variety of sources. It is important that the layout operator be able to identify the format at a glance.

We use the following extensions at New Riders Publishing:

File type:	Extension:
ASCII	.TXT
DCA	.DCA
MS-Word	.DOC
Multimate	.MM
WordPerfect	.WP
WordStar	.WS
Xerox Writer	.XWP
Xywrite	.XYW

Here's how you'd name the first text file in chapter one if you had written it in MS-Word:
    MD01.DOC

And here's how it would look if you had created it in WordStar:
    MD01.WS

The only trick to using extensions is to make sure that every format has a unique code. Some word processors automatically assign a default extension. Use that default if possible. Don't, however, allow files in two different formats to share the same extension, even if it means renaming files after typing them in.

Applying the system to other documents

To this point, we've explored a simple naming system for books. But what about magazines, newsletters, and marketing materials, which are rarely divided into convenient chapters?

The easiest way to adapt the system to recurring publications, like magazines and newsletters, is to use the numbers to indicate the issue and the last four letters to show the article or section. For instance, a newsletter might choose NL as its identifying code. If it had twelve monthly issues, every file in the January issue could start with NL01. February files would start with NL02, and so on until December, which would be NL12.

Daily, weekly, and biweekly publications are probably best served by using the last two digits of the issue number.

Once you've identified the issue in the file name, use the rest of the file name to indicate the article. Suppose, for instance, the newsletter typically has a lead story, a news section, an article about people who have been promoted, a masthead, and a calendar. Here's how you might name the text files for the January issue:
    NL01LEAD.DOC
    NL01NEWS.TXT
    NL01PEOP.WS
    NL01MAST.MM
    NL01CALE.XYW

(The different extensions indicate different word-processor formats, as explained above).

If this method doesn't fit the way you do business, you should be able to come up with a variation that does. For instance, you could use the letters to stand for the subject matter:
    NL01SOFT.DOC (about new software package)
    NL01CHIP.TXT (about chip shortage)
    NL01WOLF.WS (about promotion of Joseph Wolf to vice president)
    NL01MAST.MM (masthead)
    NL01CALE.XYW (calendar)

Or you could divide the publication into sections or pages, and number the articles for each:
NL01A-01.DOC
NL01A-02.TXT
NL01B-01.WS
NL01B-02.MM
NL01B-03.XYW

Use a similar method for marketing materials, proposals, etc. Elements you might want to use as identifiers include:

- product codes
- salesman's initials
- type of piece —
  brochure (BR)
  flyer (FL)
  proposal (PP)
- date
- title
- number of pages
- anything else that distinguishes one file from another

Customizing the naming system

The limitations of MS-DOS file names (eight characters plus a three-character extension) force you to think carefully about what is most important. At New Riders, the project, the chapter, and the file format represent the most crucial information. The examples above demonstrate these priorities.

If your company has different priorities, modify the naming system to match. Perhaps all your writers use the same word processor, so you already know what format the file will be in. Or perhaps you store each project in a separate subdirectory (or folder on the Macintosh) on the central file server. In that case, the location of the file would indicate the project. You might not need to include that information in the file name.

A WORD OF CAUTION: If you have several project subdirectories on the central file server, be careful about saving files to generic names, like 01.DOC, FR.CHP, etc. Although these adequately distinguish the files when they are stored in a subdirectory, you can errantly overwrite a file of the same name in another subdirectory.

Here are examples of information some companies consider important enough to indicate with code letters or numbers in their file names:

- Version number or revision level
- Dates
- Authors
- Production phase (first draft, edit, peer review, camera-ready, etc.)
- Department

Let's discuss the last two items by way of example. Many companies hand off a document to a new department when it moves from one phase to another. For instance, a software manual might move from writing, to editing, to illustration, to layout, to print. In some cases, companies mark this hand-off by changing the file name or extension. In that fashion, anyone can tell at a glance who is responsible for the document and where it stands in the production cycle.

The precise details of your naming system don't matter, as long as 1) everyone is consistent, 2) the system doesn't allow duplications, and 3) everyone understands why and how to use it.

Applying the system to pictures
We can easily extend the naming system to work for pictures as well as for text files. Picture files are covered separately in Chapter Three, "Creating Pictures."

Locating files
This section discusses how to handle text files for maximum efficiency. You've already seen how to set up a file-naming system. You can also boost productivity by standardizing where and how you locate those files.

Standardization is especially crucial for workgroups using a local area network (LAN). However, it also makes life simpler in *sneaker-net* installations — workgroups without a LAN where files are moved by carrying disks from one computer to the other. A simple location system makes it easy for one person to find a file on someone else's machine.

A standard hard disk structure is perhaps most important for users of Xerox Ventura Publisher, whether or not they work on a network. To speed things up, they should set up identical subdirectories on all computers. The *pointers* (instructions that tell Ventura where to look for text, picture and style files) in Ventura's chapter files will be correct on any machine. Operators can then use MS-DOS to copy and move files between machines, instead of Ventura's ponderous Multi-Chapter copy facility.

We will use the MS-DOS and Unix term *subdirectory* to refer to the subdivisions on a hard disk. Subdirectories correspond to the *folders* on a Macintosh.

Naming and organizing subdirectories

The simplest, most straightforward way to organize a hard disk for desktop publishing is to create a separate subdirectory for each project. Put every file relating to that project in the same subdirectory. In that fashion, you can backup the entire project just by copying the contents of that subdirectory.

We also favor a simple method of naming subdirectories. We use the same two-letter code that identifies the book as a whole. Thus, we would place a book with the code MD into a subdirectory called \MD.

Larger projects may require subdivision. For instance, New Riders' computer books include hundreds of pictures. Putting all these pictures in the same spot as the text files would crowd the directory. For this reason, we create a separate subdirectory for the pictures. If the text files are stored in the subdirectory \MD, then the pictures go into \MD\PIX.

The use of the same code name minimizes confusion (Let's see — was that subdirectory called NEWSLET? Or was it NEWS? Or NEWSLETS?) Short names also keep typing to a minimum. Most of all, we like this procedure because we don't have to maintain a separate list of subdirectory names. Everybody who works on a project has to know the two-letter code anyway (so they can recognize files). There's no danger the crew won't know the correct name for the subdirectory.

Locating backups

Deciding where to put backup copies can also be simple and straightforward. Allot one file drawer (or a portion of one) for each project. Create one file folder for each chapter or section. In that folder, put the latest hard copy printout, and the latest floppy disk backup. Personnel who work on the chapter remove the file, keeping it until they have completed their revisions. They are then responsible for updating the backup disk and returning the file to its place at the end of the day.

Typing guidelines

If you establish clear typing guidelines, getting the text file from the word processor into the page-layout program is simple and straightforward. If you do not, your authors' efforts to help may make things worse instead of better. In most cases, it's just as easy for them to do things the right way — provided they know your needs in advance.

The *right way* varies from system to system. Obviously, you should modify the examples we give to fit your situation. Although the specific *solutions* vary, the *problems* tend to remain the same from system to system. As you assemble a tool kit for writers and authors, be sure to address these 12 issues:

1. General format concerns
2. Text attributes
3. Special characters
4. Indents
5. Tabs versus spaces
6. Tables

7. Lists

8. Pictures

9. Headers and footers

10. Indexing and footnotes

11. Hyphenation

12. Dating files

These problem areas are explained in more detail below. Page-layout programs differ greatly. We can't give you specific suggestions. We can, however, spotlight the trouble areas and warn you to decide in advance how to handle them. If you take these precautions, the transition from word processing to page layout can be smooth and painless. Otherwise, you may spend unnecessary hours converting and cleaning up files.

General format concerns

Most page-layout programs can retain formatting from text files in some form or another. In some cases, they preserve the actual style sheets and fonts from the word processor. In other cases, they allow you to specify the format with *tags* — brief codes in the manuscript (Figure 2-3).

Few page-layout programs, however, can translate all of a word processor's formatting. Indeed, if writers use too many word-processor commands, they can make things more difficult.

So here's the crux of the problem — and a solution: It's up to you to determine exactly what writers should and shouldn't include in text files and to tell them in advance.

In many cases, this means writers should do *less* formatting in the word processor. When using Xerox Ventura Publisher, for instance, word-processor formatting commands make things harder for the layout operator. For example, if the writer centers text, the layout operator has to take out the extra spaces before centering it properly in Ventura. Or if the writer types in something to represent a bullet, the layout operator has to delete it before inserting a true typographic bullet.

```
@BODYFIRST = This chapter is
devoted to the mechanics of
producing a text file. It con-
tains suggestions that make it
easier and faster to turn a raw
manuscript into a finished docu-
ment. It does not deal with
grammar, usage, or style. Those
aspects of writing are covered
in Chapters Six and Seven.
We divided the chapter into
three sections:
@LISTROUND = file handling tips
- -<R><I>how to name and or-
ganize files for efficiency and
productivity<D>
@LISTROUND = typing guidelines -
 -<R><I>how to keyboard text so
the resulting file merges
smoothly into the page layout<D>
@LISTROUND = preformatting tech-
niques - -<R><I>how to speed
production by doing part of the
formatting directly in the text
file<D>
```

Tags

2–3. Some page-layout programs allow you to specify the format inside the text file by using codes, often called tags.

Figure 2-4 shows a list of formatting rules for Xerox Ventura Publisher. You should create a similar summary for your page-layout program.

Text attributes

Most page-layout programs can import text attributes like bold, italics, and underline from the word processor. Some can bring in font changes as well. For maximum efficiency, you must tell your writers when to

Formatting rules for text files

- Type everything flush left.
- Put a single carriage return between paragraphs.
- Put a single space after periods, colons, and question marks.
- Do not justify.
- Do not center.
- Do not indent.
- Do not use temporary margins.
- Do not insert bullets or numbers in lists.
- Do not use tab stops between columns (type each entry as a separate paragraph).
- Do not use bold or italics *unless* you are indicating a word or phrase within an otherwise normal paragraph. For instance, do not bold headings and subheadings.
- Do not type headings or subheads in all caps.

2–4. General formatting rules for text files that will be imported into Xerox Ventura Publisher. You should create a similar list of rules for your program.

assign attributes to text in the word processor, and when to leave them up to the layout operator.

We use Ventura Publisher at New Riders. The only time we want writers to use text attributes is to italicize a word or phrase within a paragraph. We prefer to do everything else ourselves. That way, if we decide to change the look of first-level headings, we can do so with a single command in the page-layout program. If we relied on the authors to format headings, we'd have to change each one individually.

By contrast, many Macintosh users ask authors to format all the main elements — headings, subheadings, body text — exactly as they will appear in the final document.

The list below highlights some of the main issues. For each of these page elements, you must tell writers whether or not to use text attributes:

- chapter titles
- headings
- subheadings
- body text
- italics, bold, or underline within a paragraph
- notes and warnings
- font changes (for instance, a typewriter-style font to indicate what readers see on the computer screen)

In addition to telling authors *when* to use text attributes, you must also tell them *how* to achieve them. For instance, if writers want to italicize a phrase within a paragraph, should they use the word processor's native italics command? Or should they use a special code instead? And if you expect them to specify fonts, they must know the styles, sizes, and codes in advance.

Special characters

The standard computer keyboard doesn't contain all the symbols and characters essential for a typeset document. Since these characters do not appear on the keyboard, you must tell authors how and when to insert them into their manuscripts.

The specifics will vary depending on your word processor and page-layout program. Many Macintosh word processors, for instance, can insert typographic characters directly into the text file. These characters will survive importation into the page-layout program. By contrast, many MS-DOS word processors cannot directly insert typographic characters in a fashion that will be recognized by the page-layout program.

Regardless of the specifics, list the most important characters and tell authors how to achieve them. Table 2-1, for instance, shows an example for Xerox Ventura Publisher users. Ventura accommodates typographic characters by way of bracket codes. Notice the extra column on the right for users to note keyboard shortcuts in Ventura.

Table 2-2 shows the same idea for users of Microsoft Word on the Macintosh (for importation into programs like PageMaker and Quark Xpress). You should build a similar table for your writers.

Table 2-1: A partial listing of typographic characters available through bracket codes

Character	Symbol	Code	Keyboard Shortcut
open quote	"	<169>	Ctrl-Shift-[
close quote	"	<170>	Ctrl-Shift-]
em dash	—	<197>	Ctrl-]
en dash	–	<196>	Ctrl-[
copyright	©	<189>	Ctrl-Shift-C
registered	®	<190>	Ctrl-Shift-R
trademark	™	<191>	Ctrl-Shift-2
bullet	•	<195>	
cents	¢	<155>	
pounds (British)	£	<156>	
yen	¥	<157>	
section	§	<185>	
paragraph	¶	<188>	
ellipsis	…	<193>	
non-breaking space		<N>	
line break		<R>	

Table 2-2: A partial listing of typographic characters available in Microsoft Word on the Macintosh

Character	Symbol	Keystroke Combination
open quote	"	Option-[
close quote	"	Option-Shift-[
em dash	—	Option-Shift- -
en dash	–	Option- -
copyright	©	Option-g
registered	®	Option-r
trademark	™	Option-2
bullet	•	Option-8
cents	¢	Option-4
pounds (British)	£	Option-3
yen	¥	Option-y
section	§	Option-6
paragraph	¶	Option-7
ellipsis	...	Option-;
non-breaking space		Option-Shift
line break		Command-Shift-KeyboardEnter

You will notice three important typographic symbols at the top of the lists: open quotes, close quotes, and em dashes. We include them for information purposes. Most page-layout programs can convert these characters. To create open and close quotes, writers can use the standard inch marks (") on the computer keyboard. To create an em dash, they can type two hyphens (- -). The page-layout program will automatically convert these characters into typographic symbols when it loads the file.

Still, the conversion routines are not perfect. Some writers need to use these symbols in an unconventional fashion that will not convert. For this reason, we recommend including them on your list.

Accuracy: The vice of being right.

Indents
Specify whether or not authors should indent paragraphs, excerpts, long quotes, and similar material. In some page-layout programs, it is better to type this material normally, so the layout operator can make the decisions. If you want authors to do the work, tell them precisely when and how to indent.

Tabs versus spaces
If authors will be asked to indent material or type in tabular tables, they must understand the difference between tabs and spaces. Page-layout programs require true tabs. A true tab stop can *jump* horizontally. Some word processors insert spaces in place of a tab. When you import these spaces into the page-layout program, they will not format correctly.

Be sure to let authors know how and when to insert tabs.

Tables
Tables are a complex topic. Each program uses own approach.

On the Macintosh side, some publishers treat tables like pictures. They create the table with a separate application, then import it into the page-layout program. Conversely, some people use tab stops.

With Ventura Publisher on the IBM PC, you can legitimately use at least four different approaches to format tables:

- spaces with monospaced fonts
- tab stops
- side-by-side paragraphs
- table mode (Professional Extension only)

Determine in advance how you plan to handle tables. Then tell authors in advance how to format their text files to match your system.

If authors build their tables with spreadsheet programs, they must also know how to convert the spreadsheet output to a file format the page-layout program can understand. Some desktop-publishing programs can read spreadsheet files directly. In other cases, however, the spreadsheet must be printed to a disk file to convert it to ASCII format. In many cases, you must also take additional steps to insert true tab stops between columns (instead of spaces) before you can properly format the table.

You must also tell authors how to title, caption, and number tables.

Lists

Lists are another potential problem area. You must tell authors how to type them so the layout operator 1) knows what kind of list it is supposed to be and 2) doesn't have to do any extra work to clean up or convert the list. For instance, at New Riders, we use both bullet lists and numbered lists. We instruct writers *not* to insert the bullets or the numbers, since that is done automatically in Ventura Publisher. We do, require, however, that they tag the list correctly so the layout operator knows what type of list it is. We treat definition lists and other more complex lists as tables.

If you want authors to format lists inside the word processor, then you must explain such things as how to create a bullet character, how large the character should be, how much space to put after the bullet, how much to indent the rest of the item, how much space to put before, after, and between items, and so on.

Pictures

Handling pictures in the text file has two aspects: 1) a reference in the main text and 2) a mark in the manuscript providing additional information for the layout operator.

Those of you who produce short, simple documents won't need to take these extra steps for pictures. But if you have more than 10 pictures per document, you'll want to address the issues outlined in this section. Failure to do so will slow you down at the layout stage.

The first step is to formulate a rule for text references. When and how should authors refer to pictures in the main text?

For technical documents and books, the rule should be to include a text reference for every picture. For example:
> Table 1-3 shows the six most frequent problems and the steps you can take to correct them.
> A chapter file contains pointers to many other files (see Figure 3-2).

Tell authors in advance how you want them to handle these issues:

- Where to place the name of the illustration. Choices include within parentheses at the end of the sentence, or inside the sentence itself.

- Whether to capitalize and/or abbreviate words like *figure*, *table*, and *illustration*.

- Whether to put the actual numbers in, or to leave that for the layout phase.

- How to number illustrations. Most books use dual numbering: chapter number, hyphen, figure number. Thus, Figure 10-17 would refer to the 17th illustration in chapter ten.

- Whether it is permissible to say "the figure on this page" or otherwise indicate the exact location. We recommend against it, since the layout operator may be forced to place the picture somewhere else.

In addition to text references, you may also want authors to mark the spot where they'd like the illustration to appear, and/or to give more information about the picture.

Marking picture location is of less concern to those who produce newsletters, magazines, and marketing materials. In those applications, the editors and production people usually make the decisions about artwork.

In books and technical documents, on the other hand, it is often crucial to know which picture the author had in mind. In its most basic form, marking pictures can be as simple as adding a line in the text:
> Put the picture of the space shuttle here.

However, if you have more than 10 or so pictures per chapter, you'll probably need a more sophisticated system. At New Riders, we often have dozens of pictures per chapter, each contained in a separate electronic file.

Layout operators would go crazy trying to guess which pictures were which, so our system includes the file names too. The operators know at a glance which electronic file to use for the picture.

We even go so far as to ask authors to type in a description and a suggested caption. The caption is tagged by the author, so all the layout operator has to do is cut it from the main text and paste it into the caption frame.

Regardless of the page-layout program you use, you should be able to set up a similar system to streamline the inclusion of pictures. Turn to Chapter Three, *Creating Pictures*, for more on how to name and mark pictures in the text file.

Headers and footers

Most page-layout programs cannot accept header and footer information from a word processor. Your writers will be wasting their time, and may even complicate matters, if they try to include this information. In most cases, you should instruct authors not to include any page numbers in the text file. You will accomplish this later in the page-layout phase.

Indexing and footnotes

Those of you who produce longer documents must be sure to tell writers how to handle footnotes and indexing. If you do not, you are likely to waste time. Authors will insert commands in the word processor, not realizing that they cannot be converted by the page-layout program.

That doesn't mean that authors can't and shouldn't help with these tasks. Some page-layout programs can accept indexing and footnoting commands, provided they are typed in the correct format. Simply be sure to inform authors in advance, so they don't waste time entering information in an incompatible form.

Hyphenation

Most page-layout programs accomplish hyphenation on their own, separately from the word-processing program. Hyphenating in the word processor is usually a waste of time.

However, you may want to insert discretionary hyphens for certain unusual words that might otherwise be broken incorrectly. Discretionary hyphens tell the page-layout program "don't hyphenate this word unless you have to, but if it becomes necessary, here's where I want the hyphen to appear." In many cases, it's as important to tell the program what *not* to hyphenate. For instance, you probably do not want to hyphenate the names of your company and its products.

Realistically, though, a better strategy is to enter these special words into the exception dictionary of the page-layout program, so they will be always be handled correctly.

Dating files

It is important to keep an accurate record of revisions. Otherwise, editors may accidentally use an old version, or copy an old file on top of a new one. To prevent this, some companies date their files.

You may feel that the dating capabilities of your operating system are sufficient to keep things straight. Or you may leave dating to a desktop-publishing utility. Or you may choose to put the date into the file name. If none of these methods works, consider placing dating information into the file itself.

At New Riders, for instance, we ask authors to place a specially tagged line at the beginning of every document. This line contains the name of the text file and the date it was last worked on. In the word processor, it looks something like this:

```
@DATEMARK = PW05.DOC January 31, 1989
```

Once we bring the file into the page-layout program, we make this line invisible in the main text. However, because of the capabilities of Xerox Ventura Publisher, we are able to access the information and make it appear in a special footer. We place this footer outside the crop marks, so it will be trimmed off after printing. Nonetheless, it appears at the bottom of every page. Editors can tell at a glance whether they have the latest version (Figure 2-5).

Locating files 2 – 25

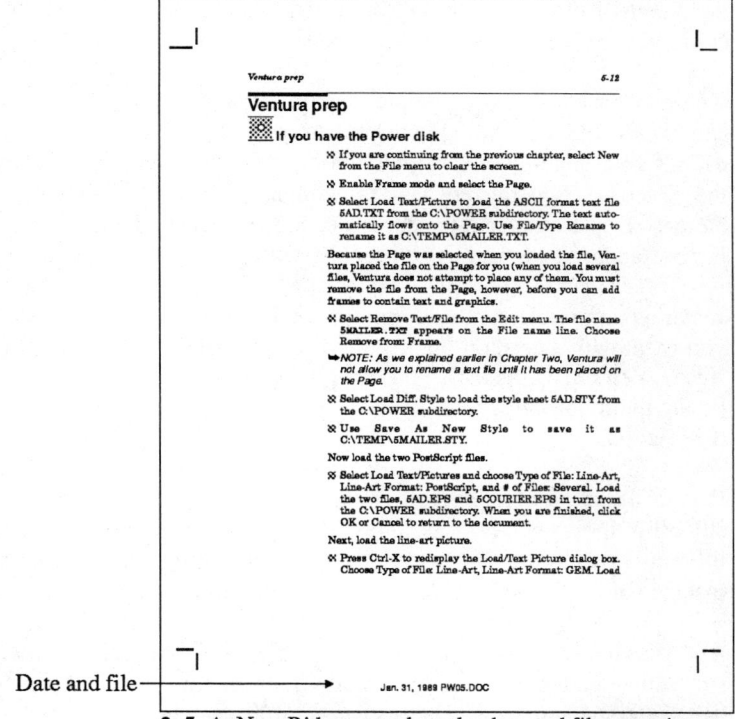

2–5. At New Riders, we place the date and file name into a special footer that appears outside the crop marks. (Date and file → Jan. 31, 1989 PW05.DOC)

Preformatting text files

So far you've seen how to improve operations by creating a naming system and establishing typing guidelines. Those who want the maximum in desktop-publishing efficiency should also take a third step. They should ask authors to preformat their text files.

The concept behind preformatting is very simple. You ask authors to code their manuscript in some fashion, so they are doing much of the formatting for you. It is not appropriate if you work with a wide variety of short documents from different authors. Under such conditions, you should count yourself lucky just to get a reasonably clean text file.

On the other hand, if you prepare long documents with a set format, you can boost efficiency through preformatting. And preformatting can work even if your page-layout program doesn't use style sheets. For instance, the Standard Generalized Markup Language (SGML) in use by the Defense Department and the aerospace industries is nothing more than a list of standard code names you can use with any typesetting system.

Just how you implement preformatting will depend on your software. If you work with a desktop-publishing program that uses style sheets (like Xerox Ventura Publisher), you can give authors a tag list, so they can pretag the manuscript. We'll show you an example of a tag list later in this section.

If your desktop-publishing program doesn't have style sheets, you can still ask authors to insert brief codes. Then you can use the search function in your word-processing or desktop-publishing program to locate each instance of a code and replace it with the correct formatting commands.

And if you have a word processor/page layout combination that works smoothly together, you can distribute a list of formatting rules (font styles and sizes, spacing, etc.). Authors can set titles, headings, text, and other page elements in the proper format right from the beginning, with the assurance that the style will pass through. For instance, PageMaker and Microsoft Word can work together in this fashion.

Preformatting has pros and cons. On the plus side, it can bring dramatic cost savings for long, complex documents. On the down side, it requires a training process before authors can get up to speed. In addition, a coded manuscript may be harder to proofread.

> *I like to leave out the parts that people skip.*
> Elmore Leonard

If you want authors to help you out with preformatting, you'll have to give them the tools. At a minimum, they will need:

- a list of the correct codes and instructions on how to use them
- visual examples of each format, so they can see the end results
- tips on how to speed the process with keyboard macros and other tricks

Creating a list of codes

The first step in preformatting is to create a list of codes, so authors know what, when, and how to insert them into the manuscript.

If your authors work with WYSIWYG (what you see is what you get) word processors, this list may contain visual samples plus the essential spacing and font attributes. If you are working on a non-WYSIWYG system, like most PC word processors, the list will contain the codes the authors must insert.

We will briefly describe the list we use at New Riders. Although we work with Ventura Publisher, you could easily adapt these principles for other programs. Ventura works with codes in the text file, called *tags*. Consider, for example, the first few lines of an imaginary manuscript:

```
Passion's Pure Pillage
It was a dark and stormy night. Vivian
gazed achingly at the fire. The logs were
dying to embers, like the embers of their
love. Softly she sighed his name: "Dirk.
Oh Dirk!" Would she ever gaze into his
soft yet manly eyes again?
```

Until we tell it otherwise, Ventura treats everything in the file like body text. To signal Ventura to treat these lines differently, you insert codes:

```
@HEADCHAP = Passion's Pure Pillage
@BODYFIRST = It was a dark and stormy
night. Vivian gazed achingly at the fire.
The logs were dying to embers, like the
embers of their love. Softly she sighed
his name: "Dirk. Oh Dirk!" Would she ever
gaze into his soft yet manly eyes again?
```

When the layout operator brings in this pretagged text, Ventura instantly formats it:

Passion's Pure Pillage

*I*t was a dark and stormy night. Vivian gazed achingly at the fire. The logs were dying to embers, like the embers of their love. Softly she sighed his name: "Dirk. Oh Dirk!" Would she ever gaze into his soft yet manly eyes again?

But to pretag text in Ventura, authors must follow two rules. First, they must use the correct format. Second, they must use the same names we use at New Riders, and spell them correctly.

Our author's handbook teaches them the format. Then we give them a tag list which summarizes the names and spellings. Here is the tag list we distribute to our authors at New Riders (Table 2-3).

Table 2-3: New Rider's Tag List

Tag Name	Macro	Description
Body Text and variations		
BodyBold		bold face for emphasis in short paragraphs
BodyCourier		text seen/entered by reader
BodySetIn		set in from left margin
Body Text		default condition, do not pretag
Captions		
Z_Caption		picture caption
Callouts		
Z_Box Text		callouts
Headings and Titles		
Head1		first level heading
Head2		second level heading
Head3		third level heading
HeadChap		chapter title, follows chapter number
HeadChapNum		chapter number
Lists		
List2Col1		2-column list with bullet, first column
List2Col2		2-column list with bullet, second column
ListBoxHollow		hollow box bullet
ListBoxSolid		solid box bullet
ListNum		auto-numbered list
ListRound		round bullet
Notes		
Note		important information
NoteWarn		warning of dangerous condition
Other		
PictureMark		picture location marker
Tables		
TableHead		title of a table
Z_Tbl_Beg		beginning of a table
Z_Tbl_End		end of table

Creating visual examples

In addition to giving authors a list of codes, you should also show them what the results will look like. This can be as simple as taking a previous document and circling examples of each key page element. At New Riders, we go one step further. We build what we call a tag dictionary. This listing not only shows what the page elements look like, it also gives advice on how and when to use each one.

Figure 2-6 shows a sample page from our tag dictionary. Chapter Eight provides our entire dictionary for those of you who would like to use it as a model for one of your own. The dictionary is also on the optional Managing disk.

Why go to the trouble of building a dictionary? You'll find that authors do a better job of writing and coding if they can visualize what things look like. In addition, a tag dictionary reminds authors of the possibilities at their disposal. Some writers may not use such things as bulleted lists, numbered lists, tables, or multi-level headings unless you show them how.

Speeding the preformatting process

Up to this point, we've told you how to preformat, but we haven't suggested how to go about it. You can make this job easier for authors by providing them with macros, templates, and other aids.

If you preformat with codes, you'll find them easier, faster and more accurate to enter with keyboard macros. If you look back at the sample tag list shown earlier, you will notice a space for authors to jot down the macro they wish to use.

Many leading word processors have built-in macro processors and/or glossary functions. If yours does not, there are numerous programs that add this capability to PC and Macintosh word processors. New Riders even goes to the lengths of providing predefined macros to authors, to make things even easier.

If macros don't seem to be the answer, you may prefer to work with templates. For example, if you use Quark Xpress, you could ask your writers to work with QuarkStyle, the compatible word-processing pro-

Locating files

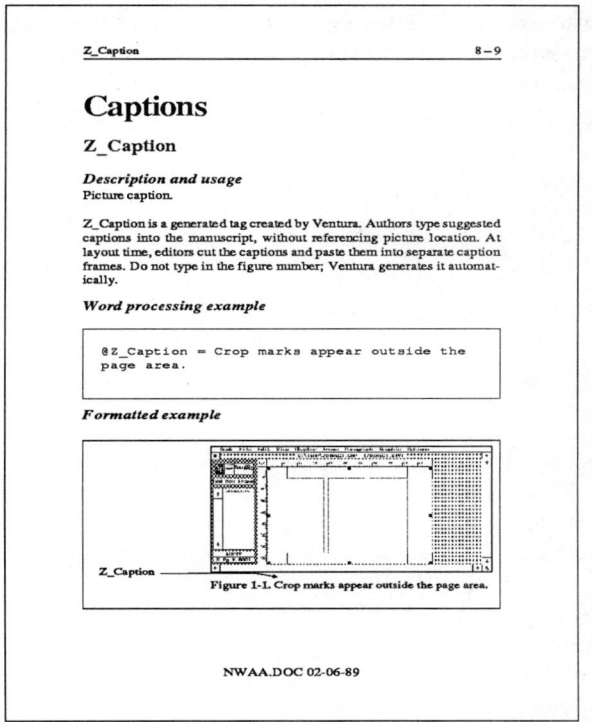

> **Z_Caption**   8—9
>
> # Captions
>
> ### Z_Caption
>
> **Description and usage**
> Picture caption.
>
> Z_Caption is a generated tag created by Ventura. Authors type suggested captions into the manuscript, without referencing picture location. At layout time, editors cut the captions and paste them into separate caption frames. Do not type in the figure number; Ventura generates it automatically.
>
> **Word processing example**
>
> ```
> @Z_Caption = Crop marks appear outside the
> page area.
> ```
>
> **Formatted example**
>
> [screenshot showing Z_Caption pointing to "Figure 1-1. Crop marks appear outside the page area."]
>
> NWAA.DOC 02-06-89

2–6. The New Riders tag dictionary lets authors see how each page element will look in the final version. It also gives advice on when, how, and why to preformat.

gram from the same company. Your layout operator would build a template using Quark Xpress. Authors could then access and use that template via QuarkStyle. And templates will work with almost any program, whether WYSIWYG or code-based.

> *The less people know about how sausages and books are made, the better they'll sleep at night.*

Those who use a code-based system may also want to experiment with ways to hide the codes. Some word processors feature a hidden text feature that allows you to hide and show codes at will. Show them when you need to make changes, and hide them when you want to proofread.

An author's tool kit

As noted earlier, the first part of your job is designing systems that work. The second part is convincing (as in motivating, conniving, begging, or forcing) people to use those systems.

You'll get much more cooperation from writers and authors if you provide them with a tool kit — a selection of hints, tips, aids, and examples. Here are some of the things you should consider for your tool kit. Beneath each item, we've listed the chapter(s) in this book where you can find an explanation or example. To make the list more complete, we've also included some items that don't have to do with the mechanics of creating files, but that do belong in every writer's arsenal.

- File-naming system
  Chapter Two, Chapter Three

- File-location guidelines (subdirectory/folder names)
  Chapter Two, Chapter Three

- Typing guidelines (including format, special characters, and text attributes)
  Chapter Two

- Tag list or formatting settings
  Chapter Two, Chapter Five, Chapter Eight

- Tag dictionary
  Chapter Two, Chapter Five, Chapter Eight

- Macros for preformatting
  Chapter Two

- Templates for preformatting
  Chapter Two, Chapter Five

- Grammar and usage guide
  Chapter Six

- Writing guide
  Chapter Seven
- Spelling and capitalization glossary
  Chapter Four, Chapter Six

Creating Pictures

3

In the last chapter, you learned efficient ways to create text files for desktop publishing. This chapter explains how to create pictures:

- why, when, and how to create pictures
- how to name and locate picture files
- how to mark pictures in the text file
- how to caption pictures

This chapter does not explain how to operate graphics software. Nor does it cover methods of drawing or illustration. Instead, it concentrates on how to integrate pictures into the workflow. It recommends setting up standard procedures that make it simpler and faster for a workgroup to interact.

Many of these techniques will save you time and trouble even if you're a sole practitioner who seldom has more than one or two pictures per document. On the other hand, some of them would be overkill for a small operation. As with all the chapters in this book, it's up to you to decide which ones are appropriate for the way you like to work.

Several problems can crop up when you add pictures to the equation:

- The layout operator doesn't know which pictures belong where.
- The pictures are the wrong size, or the wrong file format.
- The project is delayed because the pictures were started too late.

You probably won't be surprised to learn that our recommended solution is to *plan ahead*. You can easily create a tool kit for authors, illustrators, and layout operators to speed and simplify the picture-building process. The suggestions in this chapter will get you started.

Why and when to create pictures

Pictures, charts, graphs, and tables make technical documents more user-friendly. Some people learn through words; others learn visually. Technical documents should serve both. Pictures can even save writing time. A single picture can convey relationships that would take pages to explain. In addition, pictures improve shelf appeal. They make books, newsletters, magazines, and marketing materials more appealing.

In short documents like magazines and newsletters, pictures are often added after the fact. The editor or art director may have the job of inventing ways to dress up the articles.

In longer documents, however, pictures often play a more crucial role. For instance, they may contain precise technical material. In such cases, it's essential to get the *right* pictures at the right spot. In addition, it's important to get started early with pictures, so they don't delay the production of the document.

When to create pictures

If you ask us when to start producing pictures, our answer is *the sooner the better*. Far too many desktop-publishing projects are delayed because people underestimate the time it takes to find and format pictures. In some cases, the best strategy is to write the text to conform to the illustrations — not the other way around.

But if you ask us when to integrate the pictures into the final layout, then our answer is *the later the better*. We believe the best way to handle pictures is to keep them separate from the text until the last minute. Otherwise your layout operator can waste time formatting pictures that may be deleted, resized, changed, or rearranged.

A question arises if you keep the pictures separate from the text. How do you compare the pictures to text references to check for accuracy? As you will read later in this chapter, we recommend naming each picture and noting in the manuscript where it belongs. Editors can then compare the manuscript side-by-side with a separate picture printout.

How to create pictures

A desktop publisher has several ways to get illustrations into a document:

- electronic art
- scanned art
- traditional line drawings
- photographs

In this section, we'll give you some tips that apply to any type of artwork. The trick is to experiment until you discover which formats, sizes, and techniques work best. Then you can create standards for authors, illustrators, and layout personnel. A deceptively simple idea — yet far too many desktop publishers fail to create picture standards. They reinvent the wheel for each new project.

General rules for electronic art

There's nothing wrong with using traditional cut-and-paste methods to create illustrations for a desktop-published document. We recommend doing whatever is most efficient (even if you have to hide your scissors and paste in the drawer afterward).

Still, most desktop publishers prefer to work with electronic illustrations, which offer time and efficiency advantages. Five general rules apply to electronic art:

1. Start with a thumbnail sketch.
2. Create it separately from the page-layout process (if possible).
3. Put each picture into a separate file.
4. Name files according to a standard system.
5. Make the picture as close as possible to its final size.

All of these rules have exceptions, so let's discuss them in more detail.

A thumbnail sketch is nothing more than a rough drawing of your intended picture. It's not required if you are working with an existing drawing. But if you are creating artwork from scratch — whether charts, graphs, illustrations, or technical drawings — you can save time and trouble with a thumbnail.

Creating a thumbnail sketch forces you to do the decision-making up front. It's the equivalent of making an outline before you start to write. The appearance doesn't matter, so don't avoid thumbnails because you flunked third-grade art class. What is important is that you make as many choices as possible before you start, so you don't get bogged down during the process.

Most page-layout programs have some drawing features. Nevertheless, you should create electronic art with a separate package when possible. Standalone drawing programs permit more sophisticated drawings. In addition, they allow you to save the results as a separate file — something that's not possible with every page-layout program. For instance, drawings created in Ventura Publisher cannot be exported to other documents in any simple fashion. For all intents and purposes, they are trapped inside the original document.

That's not to say you should never use the illustration capabilities of a page-layout program. However, your operation will be more efficient if you are set up to handle pictures on a separate track from the page layout.

Saving each picture as a separate file makes it easier to mix, match, copy, move, delete, and rearrange pictures. It also lets you reuse a picture in another document, or as the starting point for a new illustration.

Those of you who use tables and charts as illustrations may want to break this rule, depending on your page-layout program. Some programs have table-editing features that let you easily include tables right in the middle of the text stream. However, most programs perform better if tables are treated and placed as standalone illustrations.

Most desktop publishers will also benefit from a standard naming system for pictures. We will suggest a detailed procedure below. In summary, it should be a simple, straightforward method that ties into the system you use for text files and document files. However, if you rarely use more than one or two pictures, you may find a standard system unnecessary.

Finally, we suggested above that you create pictures as close as possible to the same size as the final document. That is good advice for many pictures, since it minimizes the distortion that can occur when pictures are resized. However, there are many cases when you cannot approximate the final size. In addition, many desktop publishers deliberately create pictures larger than the final size. Then they reduce the picture. This reduction minimizes irregularities, causing an apparent increase in smoothness and resolution.

Common illustration methods

Next we'll examine some of the most common illustration methods for desktop-published documents. Glance through this list. You may find an idea or two you've overlooked.

Drawing programs
Almost anyone can create acceptable drawings with today's graphics programs. A good illustration usually doesn't require anything fancy. Many pictures show relationships, and that's a job that can be done with boxes, circles, and arrows.

We don't have the space here to cover every drawing program on the market and how it interfaces with every page-layout program. Suffice it to say that it takes some experimentation. Our experiences with AutoCAD and Ventura Publisher may give you some insight as to the steps you can take to streamline operations.

There are at least four ways to bring an AutoCAD drawing into Ventura Publisher. At New Riders, we quickly discovered that two of these methods are the most efficient.

For most applications, we prefer drawings that have been plotted. To produce an AutoCAD vector drawing, we draw it larger than the frame it will occupy in the final document. That way, Ventura will not stretch and distort the drawing when it brings it in. We scale the drawings to twice the frame size, then we add a border and annotations. We make the annotations, text, dimensions, and symbols twice the size we want them in the finished illustration. Then we save the AutoCAD drawing and plot it to a .PLT file. We configure AutoCAD for the Hewlett-Packard 7586.

For certain other applications, PostScript output works best. PostScript has the most dimensional stability — that is, the dimensions are more likely to remain accurate. After printing to a PostScript disk file with AutoCAD, we open the file with a text editor. We manually insert several lines that convert the file into the Encapsulated PostScript format Ventura can understand.

This is just a brief summary of the methods we've worked out to make AutoCAD and Ventura work smoothly together. The point is that we took the time to experiment. Then we wrote up the results as a series of instructions for authors and illustrators.

You can save hours — even *days* — of time by settling on a drawing program and creating a set of standards for its use.

In God you should trust. Everything else... you should test.

A screen capture utility

Computer books often require sample screens (Figure 3-1). The easiest way to generate sample screens is with a capture utility. These memory-resident programs run simultaneously with the program you are documenting. When the screen looks correct, you press a key combination to take a snapshot, thereby saving a bit-map image to a disk file.

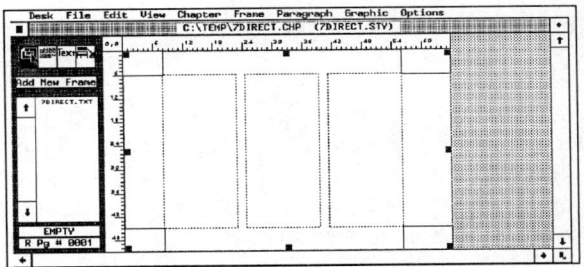

3–1. Use a screen capture utility to create sample screens like the one shown here.

At New Riders, we prefer a program called HotShot, The Graphics Editor. HotShot not only captures screens but converts file formats as well. When you capture the screen, you have an opportunity to name the file. We recommend that you use naming conventions like the ones explained later in this chapter.

When HotShot captures the screen, it saves it in its own native .HSG format. Before bringing these files into a page-layout program, you must convert them to another format. Fortunately, this is a simple batch process. Using HotShot, you flag all the files you want to convert and specify the new format. HotShot then converts them all at once.

EPS files

Computer books often need reduced-size sample pages. One way to create them is to submit full-size versions with the manuscript. These full-sized pages can then be reduced photomechanically prior to offset printing. A cheaper and easier way to produce sample pages is to use Encapsulated PostScript (EPS) files. We produced the sample pages throughout this book with EPS files.

To create an EPS file, print a page to a disk file. You can then use the EPS file like any other electronic art.

Scanned art

Scanning takes an ordinary photo or drawing and converts it into electronic form. The limitations of today's computers and laser printers means that scanned photos rarely have the quality readers expect in modern magazines, newsletters, or books. However, scanners do a good job of converting black and white line art that does not include any shades of gray.

If you want to use existing drawings, consider scanning them so you can handle them electronically rather than pasting them in. Do not consider scanning, however, if sizing is critical, since the process will introduce minor errors. It is especially important to scan the picture as close as possible to its final size, to avoid distortion.

Word-processing programs

You don't always need a drawing program to illustrate a document. You may be able to generate excellent visuals with your word processor. Long explanations impede the flow of a manuscript. Whenever possible, pull out these sections and place them in separate tables. Tables and lists make technical documents and books more valuable to the reader, since they act as a quick reference summary (Figure 3-2).

How you handle tables will depend on your software. You may be able to type them as text and use the page-layout software to generate ruling lines. Or you may need to generate them separately in a graphics package.

Confer with your layout operator about tables. Find out whether they should be typed directly into the main text file, or created as separate files. If you create them as separate files, be sure to stick to a naming system that allows them to be clearly identified. In addition, you will need to mark their location in the manuscript.

There is no abstract art. You must always start with something.
Pablo Picasso

3–2. You can often illustrate and improve a document by adding tables.

Photos

As mentioned above, scanned photographs are rarely acceptable because of the limitations of the technology. That doesn't mean, however, that you can't include photos in your documents. Simply mark where you want them to appear, then allow sufficient space on the page. In many cases, you will want to use *keylines* — boxes that indicate picture position (Figure 3-3). Be sure to tell the offset printer whether or not you want keylines to print.

Once you've positioned the pictures, you can have the printer strip in the photos using traditional techniques. Your editors or layout personnel

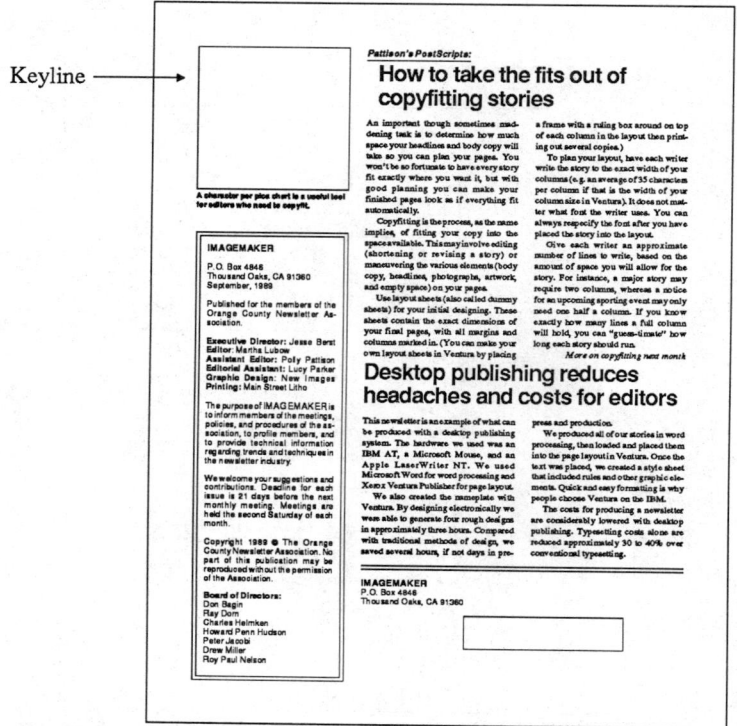

3–3. A keyline is a box that marks the location of a photograph.

should be familiar with these methods. They will need to label each picture and include cropping and sizing instructions for the printer.

A resourceful writer can obtain dozens of free photographs and drawings. Usually it is as simple as calling the marketing or public relations director. Most companies are eager to publicize their products. They are happy to grant permission if you promise to mention the product. You can also reuse text from books, newsletters, and magazines.

It is usually the author's responsibility to obtain signed permission statements for photos, drawings, and text used from other sources.

Standard picture sizes

Desktop publishing gives you the freedom to place pictures of almost any size almost anywhere on the page. But with that freedom comes confusion. By settling on a few standard picture sizes and locations, you can greatly speed the process of putting together good-looking documents.

This standardization technique is most often used by technical publishers, but it has equal validity for marketing materials, magazines, newsletters, and other design-intensive publications. In fact, the more closely you adhere to the concept of grid layouts, the more important it is that picture sizes and shapes conform to the page design.

A desktop publisher must make dozens of decisions when it comes time to place a picture:

- size
- rules around the picture (whether to use them, how many, size, margin inside rules)
- padding (spacing) around the picture
- captions (where to put them, how to format)
- labels (whether to use them, how to format)
- callouts (whether to use them, how to format)
- and many more

Why make these decisions over and over again? Figure it out once and pass out the results. Better yet, store the settings electronically, so layout operators can simply paste in the picture style they need.

We're not implying that you can't or shouldn't deviate from the standards. Almost every document will have exceptions. Your layout operators should feel free to handle unusual pictures as they see fit. But without standard sizes, *every* picture is an exception. Without standards, every picture takes extra time to size, scale, and position.

New Riders' books on Xerox Ventura Publisher typically have about six standard *frames* (our name for the box that contains the electronic picture). These standards suffice for about 90 percent of the pictures we use. Figure 3-4 shows how we distribute this information to our authors, illustrators, and layout operators.

3–4. New Riders uses standard frame sizes to reduce formatting time. You may be able to benefit by creating a similar system.

There are several viable ways to distribute this information, depending on the page-layout software and graphics software you use. You may want to give printed instructions with visual examples, similar to the ones shown here. Or you may want to provide electronic templates, so illustrators can get the correct settings just by loading your samples.

The picture printout

So far we've discussed why and how to create pictures. If you have more than a few pictures per document, we recommend an additional step: a picture printout. This printout is simply a separate document with one or more pictures per page. These pictures are labeled exactly as they are in the manuscript. Editors can proofread the text printout and the picture printout side-by-side. When the manuscript refers to a picture, the editors check it against the picture printout. They make notations and suggestions on the printout if corrections are necessary.

If you put pictures directly into the document before editing, the layout operator will have to redo much of the work. Inevitably, pictures and text get deleted and rearranged, changing the layout of pages and illustrations. If possible, try to avoid the expense and hassle of laying out a document more than once. Instead, keep the pictures separate until you are ready for the final pass.

Figure 3-5 shows a typical printout. As you can see, the key elements are the picture and an identifying name.

Naming picture files

Before desktop publishing, the author usually completed the manuscript before the artist started illustrating. It was simple to keep track of pictures back then. They could be numbered in order, with little chance that the order would change. Those same numbers would suffice to tell the paste-up artist what to put where.

In this electronic age, pictures may be created before, during, or after the manuscript. They may be produced by the author, the editor, the layout operator, an illustrator, or a combination. They may be standard photos and drawings and/or electronic files in a variety of formats. With all these options comes the potential for confusion. It is essential to arrive at a naming system you can consistently apply to any illustration, regardless of its source.

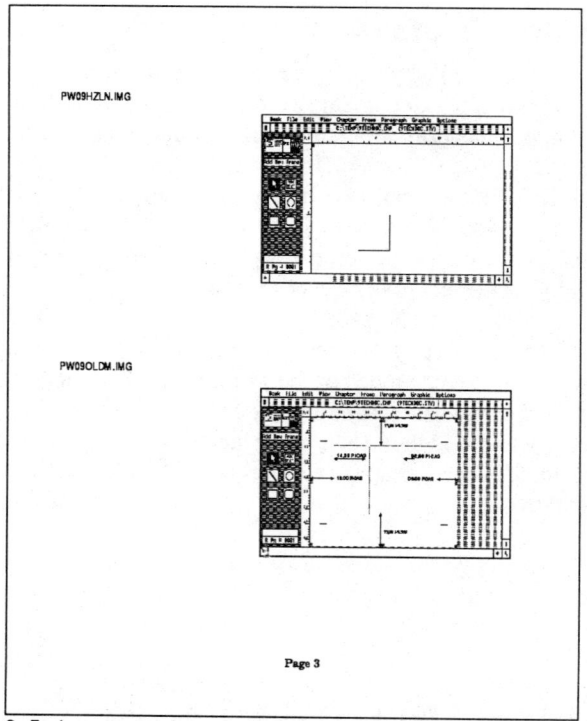

3–5. A separate picture printout saves time in the long run.

This section outlines a simple naming system for pictures. It is an extension of the system proposed in Chapter Two, "Creating Text." As you will recall, Chapter Two gave general advice on the importance and function of a naming system. This advice is equally valid for picture files. Chapter Two also described a sample system. You can extend that same system to work with picture files.

The system is designed to work within the limitations of MS-DOS. MS-DOS is the most restricted of the major operating systems. By starting with this lowest common denominator, your naming procedure will hold up even if you eventually have to transfer files between platforms.

The picture printout 3–15

MS-DOS permits eight letters in the name and three in the extension. Our sample system uses the name to describe the contents of the file and the extension to describe its format. Figure 3-6 summarizes the system as it works for text files in a book. (For hints on how this system can apply to magazines, newsletters, and marketing documents, review Chapter Two.)

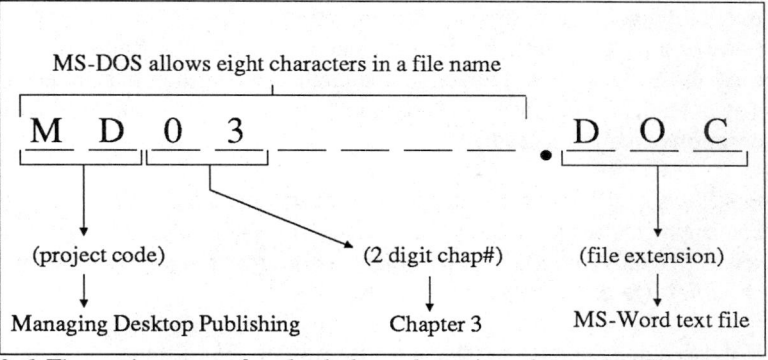

```
        MS-DOS allows eight characters in a file name

        M  D   0  3  _  _  _  _  .  D   O   C

           ↓       ↓                    ↓
      (project code)  (2 digit chap#)  (file extension)
           ↓           ↓                 ↓
   Managing Desktop Publishing  Chapter 3   MS-Word text file
```

3–6. The naming system for a book shows the project, chapter, and file type.

The fewer rules operators have to learn, the sooner they can become fully productive. In our sample naming system — which, by the way, is the one we actually use for producing our books — picture files follow the same general rules as text files. The final four letters in the name identify the picture. Thus, a picture of the Font dialog box for Chapter One might be called MD01FONT.IMG. Here's how it breaks down:

- First two characters = Project (MD)
- Second two characters = Chapter (01)
- Next four characters = Description (FONT)
- Extension = File format (.IMG)

Four characters is not a lot of space to describe a picture. In the beginning, some of us thought the system wouldn't work. In practice, however, four letters is enough to accomplish the main two jobs: 1) to give a unique name to each picture file and 2) to give at least a hint as to the contents of that picture.

When we first experimented with naming systems at New Riders, we tried numbers instead of descriptive names. The first picture in chapter one became (for instance) MD01FG01.IMG, the second picture was MD01FG02.IMG and so on.

The concept seems logical at first glance, but it breaks down in practice. Inevitably, you will find yourself rearranging pictures. The first illustration becomes the fourth one instead, and so on. If you've numbered the files, those numbers will no longer match the actual order in the chapter. The potential for confusion is enormous. Avoid numbering pictures. Use descriptive names instead.

Don't worry too much about the fact that you have only four letters to come up with a name. Use any kind of acronym or abbreviation that makes sense. The only important point is that *every picture should have a unique identifier*. Do not duplicate any names.

How do you name pictures that are very similar? For instance, a chapter in a book about Ventura might have a half-dozen screen shots of the Font dialog box, each slightly different. In such a case, you will have to use three characters as a descriptor and the fourth character to set them apart: FNTA, FNTB, FNTC, etc. The full names might be MD01FNTA.IMG, MD01FNTB.IMG, and MD01FNTC.IMG. (We recommend letters over numbers, since they allow 26 variations using only one character.)

Some manuscripts have generic pictures that are reused over and over again. You can handle this in two ways. One solution is to create a generic name by leaving out the chapter number. For instance, you might name a generic picture of the Frame menu as MDFRMENU.IMG.

You can also create copies, one for each chapter. For example, if you wanted to reuse MD01FNTA.IMG in Chapter 3, you could copy it to the name MD03FNTA.IMG. However, *never use a numbered picture from one chapter in another without renaming it.* In other words, do not use a picture called MD01PAGE.EPS in Chapter Three. Copy it under a new name first (MD03PAGE.EPS).

This same system can also accommodate tables. Some people include tables in the main text file, so there is no need for separate files. However, if you prefer to create tables as separate files, you should name them according to the same system. For instance:

- MD01TBLA.TXT
- MD01TBLB.TXT
- MD01TBLC.TXT

Picture file extensions

As with text files, we recommend using the extension to indicate the file format. The only secrets to this system are to 1) assign a unique extension to each graphic format and 2) make sure everyone uses these abbreviations. Here are the extensions we use at New Riders:

File type:	Extension:
AutoCAD slide file	.SLD
AutoCAD plot	.PLT
CGM	.CGM
Encapsulated PostScript	.EPS
GEM line art (vector)	.GEM
GEM image (bit-map)	.IMG
HotShot native graphics	.HSG
HPGL	.HPG
Lotus 1-2-3 graph	.PIC
Macintosh Paint	.PNT
Macintosh PICT	.PCT
Mentor Graphics	.PMG
PC Paintbrush	.PCX
TIFF	.TIF

Locating pictures

Chapter Two, "Creating Text," suggested a simple organizational scheme for desktop publishing. In a nutshell, every project gets its own subdirectory (folder). That subdirectory gets the same two-letter name as the project. If we assign the code MD to the book *Managing Desktop Publishing*, then we store its files in a subdirectory called \MD.

Our file-naming scheme helps this simple system hold together. Since we rigidly adhere to file conventions, we can filter out extraneous names. For instance, if we are working with chapter three, we can set the file filter to display only files that match MD03*.*, thereby eliminating anything that doesn't apply.

Still, large projects may need further subdivision. If you produce large documents with hundreds of pictures, you may want to put those pictures in their own subdirectory. At New Riders, we place picture files in a subdirectory called \PIX underneath the project subdirectory. Thus, the subdirectory for *Managing Desktop Publishing* is C:\MD, and the sub-subdirectory for pictures is C:\MD\PIX.

Marking and describing pictures in the text

For maximum efficiency, you need a simple method of marking picture locations. In this section, we will describe several ideas that may help you develop a system of your own. Here are some of the things you may be able to accomplish:

1. Create a visible mark that shows the layout operator where to put the picture.
2. Tell the layout operator which picture file to use.
3. Describe the proposed picture so the illustrator can create it.
4. Include captions, callouts, and figure numbers, so the layout operator can simply cut them and paste them into position.
5. Create a tag that automatically allocates the correct amount of space.

Some of these tasks overlap with the functions of the layout operator and are covered in more detail in Chapter Five. Still, you will probably want to assign much of this work to authors or editors. In general, they are better equipped to make decisions about pictures than the layout operator. Once they make those decisions, they need a method to pass on the information.

Just who does the marking depends on how you structure your team. At New Riders, we ask authors to mark suggested pictures in the manuscript. However, editors make the final decisions as to which pictures should go where. By the way, we have also automated the process with macros. Marking pictures in a text file is now a matter of pressing a few keys.

Let's step through the possibilities listed above and build a sample marking system.

Creating a picture mark

In its most basic form, a marking system can be as simple as "put the sales chart here." If you only have a few pictures per document, that's all you'll need to do. You can type this comment on a separate line in the text file. The layout operator can delete it and insert the picture.

Obviously, it won't always be possible to place the picture exactly where the mark is. Page layout just isn't that easy and simple. But the mark gives layout operators something to shoot for, which they can modify as conditions demand. And when the document is revised — when you add text or pictures — you'll be glad you have the marks to help you reconstruct the layout.

If you produce long documents, you'll want to do more for the layout operator than simply mention the picture. At New Riders, we have created a special format we call the PictureMark. The sole function of this tagged paragraph is to reside in the left margin and show the layout operator where each picture belongs (Figure 3-7). When we are ready to print the camera-ready chapter, we make this mark invisible by changing its color to white. (White text on a white background can't be seen.) However, the mark remains in the file, for use the next time we revise this document.

What should you use for the mark? As you can see, we use the file name of the picture. In this fashion, we've accomplished two jobs in one. Not only have we shown where the picture belongs, but we have also told the operator which file to use. This mark is originally typed into the text file (Figure 3-8), either by the author or the editor.

The
PictureMark

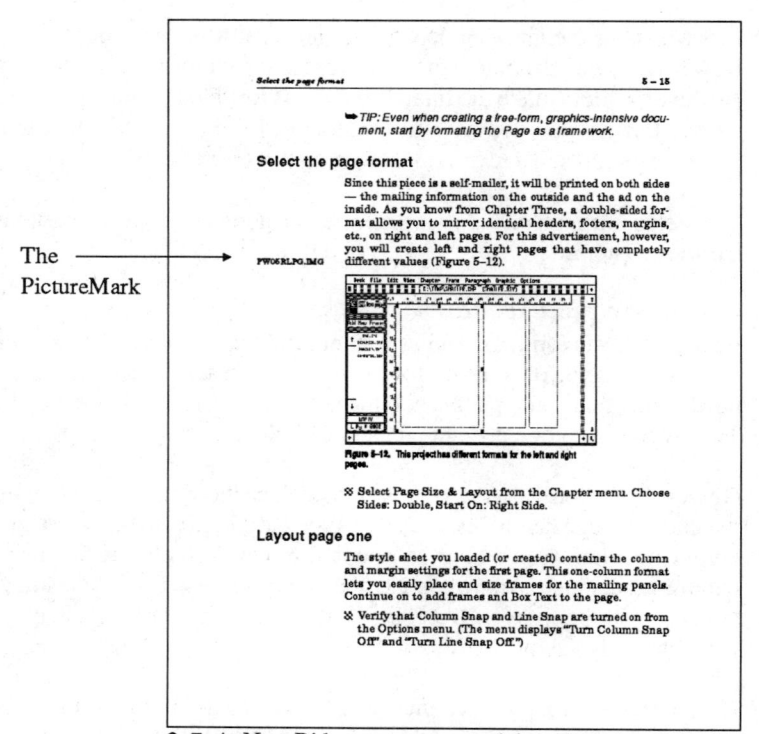

3–7. At New Riders, we use a special mark to show layout operators where to put each picture.

The PictureMark has another function. During the editing phase, we keep pictures separate from text. The PictureMark enables the editor to find and refer to pictures on the separate picture printout.

Describing the picture

If you look again at Figure 3-8, you will notice that we type more than just the PictureMark. We also include a brief description of the picture.

This description assists in the creation of the picture. Some of our authors, for instance, create their own pictures. After writing a chapter, they print it out. Then they can refer to the descriptions to remind them what to do.

In other cases, we produce the illustrations in-house. Once again, the description is a valuable aid.

```
create left and right pages
that have completely different
values (Figure 5-12).
@PICTUREMARK = PW05RLPG.IMG
SCREEN SHOT OF LEFT/RIGHT PAGES
@LISTBOXSOLID = Select Page
Size & Layout from the Chapter
```

3–8. We type the PictureMark into the directly into the text file where we want the illustration to appear.

If you place photos or illustrations into your manuscripts with traditional, cut-and-paste methods, you can also format this description to aid the paste-up artist. You could, for instance, put the description into the center of the *window* that will contain the photograph. It will provide valuable instructions to the stripper, but will be covered over when the photo is stripped in.

Captioning the picture

Some editors prefer to leave captions until last. As with all the procedures in this book, we include these ideas only as samples. You should eliminate the concepts that don't work for you and modify the others to fit your way of doing things.

For the long books we produce, layout is faster and smoother if authors and editors create the captions in advance. Then the layout operator's only job is to put the right caption with the right picture.

There are at least two ways to handle captions in advance. One idea is to include them with the separate picture printout. This method makes it easier to match up the pictures with the text. Depending on your page-layout software, you may be able to format the pictures and captions exactly as they will appear in the final document. Then you can cut the pictures from the picture printout and paste them into the final document (either electronically or manually).

You can also integrate captions into the text manuscript. If we return to the example previously shown in Figure 3-8, we could add a caption simply by typing it after the description of the picture. Figure 3-9 shows how the text file would look after the addition of this new information. (Since we use Ventura Publisher at New Riders, we also include the tag name that tells Ventura how to format the caption — in this case, the phrase @Z_CAPTION = .)

```
    create left and right pages
    that have completely different
    values (Figure 5-12).
    @PICTUREMARK = PW05RLPG.IMG
    SCREEN SHOT OF LEFT/RIGHT PAGES
    @Z_CAPTION = This project has
    different formats for the left
    and right pages.
    @LISTBOXSOLID = Select Page
    Size & Layout from the Chapter
```

3–9. You may want to try typing captions directly into the text file. The layout operator can cut them from the file and paste them into their proper locations next to the picture.

Incidentally, we use the same techniques to allow authors to type suggested callouts directly into the text file. (A callout is a label pointing to one section of an illustration.)

Allocating space

If you use manual paste-up techniques, you can still let the page-layout program do some of the work. At New Riders, we have created standard picture sizes for those situations that require manual paste-up. We then produced tags (preformatted paragraphs) to match each of those standard sizes. These paragraphs simply produce the correct amount of white space for the intended picture. We combine this spacing technique with picture marks and picture descriptions, thereby making the paste-up artist's job much easier.

How authors can help with pictures

You'll have to decide for yourselves how much the writers should help with the jobs of marking, describing, and captioning pictures. At New Riders, we ask authors to do as much as possible.

Different authors do it different ways. We don't care, as long as the first draft manuscript includes marks, descriptions, and suggested captions for the pictures. We also ask authors to include a text reference for every picture. In our opinion, almost every picture needs a text reference (such as "see Figure 1," or "refer to Figure 9-17").

It may be helpful to review two ways authors can integrate pictures into long documents. One way (probably the best) is to put in notes as they go along. As they type the manuscript, they insert notes where they want illustrations.

Adding notes is quick and simple. Still, some writers have trouble thinking about pictures while they are writing. Such writers can make a separate pass after they've finished writing. They can insert marks, descriptions, and captions during this separate pass.

No matter how they go about it, the goal is to mark each spot that needs a picture. As mentioned earlier, this task can be automated with macros. Macros make marking, describing, and captioning pictures a one-step operation. They also make it impossible to forget any part of the process.

To make your Art sparkle, polish your Craft.
                                                    Berst's Credo

An illustrator's tool kit

In previous chapters, we've made the point that people won't follow recommended procedures unless you make it easy for them. In that spirit, here are some things you should consider supplying to illustrators. Please note that in many companies, the job of creating pictures falls to authors, editors, and layout personnel. Whatever their job titles, they will probably need some of these aids. As before, we have included the chapter(s) in this book where each item is discussed.

- File-naming system
  Chapter Two, Chapter Three

- File-location guidelines (subdirectory/folder names)
  Chapter Two, Chapter Three

- Formatting guidelines — drawing guidelines, including help with sizes, formats, line widths, and output specifications
  Chapter Three

- Text guidelines — when and how to reference, mark, describe, and/or caption pictures in the text file
  Chapter Two, Chapter Three

- Macros for preformatting
  Chapter Two, Chapter Three

- Standard frame (picture) sizes and/or picture templates
  Chapter Three

Editing

4

This chapter explains how to integrate editing into the DTP workflow.

You might not think there's much new to discuss about this topic. After all, it doesn't matter how words get on paper. Whether they come from a laser printer, a typewriter, or a printing press, the editor's job remains the same: to use them to convey the message as concisely as possible.

The goal, then, remains the same — but how we get there has changed. These days, editing tasks are often done in a different order, with different tools, by different people.

This chapter contains tips and tricks for editing with minimal time and effort. Some of these techniques involve new electronic tools. But many of them are time-tested, traditional methods — methods you may not be aware of if desktop publishing has suddenly thrust you into the role of editor. We have divided this material into four sections:

- mechanics
- copyediting
- proofreading
- indexing

As with all the chapters in this book, we recommend that you skim the material with an eye towards building an editor's tool kit that fits the way you work.

The mechanics of editing

This section covers the nuts-and-bolts aspects of editing in a desktop-publishing environment, including where, when, and how to edit and how to work with the other members of the team.

Where, when, and how to edit

Until recently, there wasn't much question about where and how to edit. You did it on a typed manuscript with a red pencil. When to edit wasn't an issue either — you did it before the manuscript went to the typesetter.

Today's desktop publisher has a lot more options. Should you edit on screen or on paper? Should you edit before or after page layout? Who should enter the corrections: the editor, the author, or the layout operator?

We can't — and shouldn't — give you all the answers. You need to tailor your editing style to your own work environment. But we can recommend that you discuss these issues with the rest of the team, and decide in advance how to handle them.

Paper versus screen

Should you do your editing on the computer screen or the paper printout? We recommend that you work on screen as long as possible, provided you make at least one edit on paper before the final printout.

We recognize that most editors prefer to work on paper. So do we. You have to make adjustments and learn new skills to effectively edit electronically. But you should try hard to make this transition. If you can learn to make the first pass or two on screen, you'll boost your productivity. Electronic editing is faster than paper editing. Your changes take immediate effect. By contrast, after you edit on paper, someone must go back through and re-enter the changes.

Electronic editing also offers faster, better tools. It's easier to move big chunks of text around with cursor and keyboard than with scissors and paste. It's easier to press two keys to call up a thesaurus than it is to page through a bound volume.

Having said all that, we must warn you that you need to make at least one pass on paper. Forget all the hype about *what you see is what you get*. No matter how good your display, you'll still catch more errors on paper than you do on screen.

Word processing versus DTP

Given that on-screen editing is faster, which program should you use? We recommend that you work in the word processor as long as possible.

Some people like to run the document through the page-layout program as soon as possible. They believe that it's easier to spot mistakes when the page is in its final format.

That argument is valid. But you must balance this against the fact that most page-layout programs are deficient in editing tools. Their spell checkers are usually inferior (or non-existent). So are their search-and-replace functions and text-handling abilities.

The shorter the document, the less you need to worry about this issue. But for long, technical publications, we think you and your team will be faster if you edit in the word processor.

Don't forget that some page-layout programs can read and write to different word-processing formats. So even if authors submit text files from a different word processor, you may be able to convert them to the one you like to use for editing.

Entering corrections

Avoid duplicating effort. As mentioned above, that means doing as much of the editing on screen as possible. If possible, enter changes into the manuscript as you make them. When one person edits, and a second person enters those corrections, you increase the likelihood that errors will creep in. In addition, you've doubled the time and effort.

Still, not every editor has the power to make final decisions. Some authors demand their say over what will and won't be changed. In certain technical applications, that's a valid rule. In other cases, it may be more a question of ego. At New Riders, we submit the manuscripts to authors for their approval — but we show them the edited version only. We do not give them line by line approval over every change.

You're in for some extra work if authors insist on approving editing suggestions in advance. One way to minimize this work is to use one of the editing/commenting packages on the market. These programs allow one or more people to make suggestions and comments. These comments are treated like electronic post-it notes. They do not modify the original file until and unless the author decides to accept them. Once changes have been accepted, they don't have to be retyped. They can be made part of the manuscript with a few keystrokes. Unwanted comments are deleted just as easily.

At the very least, you can use your word processor or page-layout program to implement redlining. Redlining is the process of creating visible marks to indicate where changes have been made. That way editors and authors don't have to reread the entire manuscript. They can skim for the sections that have been changed.

If your word processor doesn't have automatic redlining, you can accomplish the same idea by putting edits in a different format (underlined, for instance, or hidden text). Again, the idea is to capture the keystrokes so they don't have to be re-entered. Once authors approve the edits, you simply change the format to match the rest of the manuscript.

Working with others

As you can see, we included *working with others* in the section on the mechanics of editing. When you set up a desktop-publishing workgroup, you're going to come up against the human interface. Solving the people issues is just as essential as figuring out the technical problems.

You and your co-workers must reach a consensus on how to work together smoothly. We've already mentioned some issues in previous chapters —

things like how to name files, where to locate them, and so on. In addition, there are many issues that relate directly to editing. Review the following items with members of your team and decide in advance how to proceed.

Standards

1. Which reference book to use for grammar questions.

Revisions

1. How to exchange drafts (on the network? on disk? on paper?).
2. How to name or mark revisions to distinguish them from previous versions.
3. Who is in the revision cycle?
4. How to assign and enforce deadlines for reviewing and returning manuscripts.
5. How to enter comments (electronically? on paper?).
6. How to identify comments (initials in the file? different type format? different color pen?).
7. Whether and how to maintain an edit history.

Corrections

1. When to enter corrections.
2. Who will enter corrections?
3. How to mark corrections (standard proofreading marks).
4. Who will check corrections to make sure they were implemented and no new errors crept in?

The thrill of literacy and the agony of delete.

Layout

1. What is the editor's responsibility (if any) for pictures, tables, and captions?
2. How and where to note corrections for format and illustrations.
3. Who converts and cleans up the word-processing file, the editor or the layout operator?

A final comment on the human issues of editing. The easiest way to be a better, faster editor is to get everyone else to do things right the first time. That's why it will be well worth your time to assemble an in-house style guide as outlined in the next section.

Copyediting

To this point, we've concentrated on the mechanics of editing. Now we are ready to turn our attention to the process of preparing a raw manuscript for publication. At New Riders, we call this process copyediting. By our definition, the job encompasses these areas:

- content
- consistency
- grammar
- style
- format

Some publishers make further distinctions. They refer to a separate process of *developmental editing* — editing for content and the big picture. They save the term *copyediting* for questions of grammar and format. We are combining these two aspects for this brief discussion. We are not, however, including proofreading — the last minute checking for typographical errors and small details. We have covered proofreading in a separate section below.

There's a lot to say about copyediting — and it's already been said in more detail than we have room for here. We refer you to the bibliography and references like Karen Judd's *Copyediting: A Practical Guide*.

But we do have space for a few suggestions about copyediting tools. These tools are especially important in a desktop-publishing work environment. Desktop publishing compresses and personalizes the traditional production process. Everything gets done faster. The manuscript is seen by fewer eyes — and that makes it easier to overlook important details. Everything gets done with fewer people — people who may be wearing a new hat (or many new hats). For these reasons, it's more important than ever to consider using the aids explained in this section.

Depending on the complexity of your publication, you may be able to combine many of these tools into a single short document. For the purposes of discussion, however, we will treat them separately. They are:

- writing guidelines
- grammar and usage guidelines
- a spelling glossary
- style lists
- copyediting checklists

You will want to distribute some of these tools to your writers. Nevertheless, they belong under the category of editing tools. Even though you pass them out to authors, they are created for the editor's benefit.

Encouragement for copyeditors

Before we step through our list of tools, a few words of encouragement to those who (to paraphrase Churchill) have had editing thrust upon them. You don't need to memorize the rules of grammar to be a good editor. Content, style, and organization will always be more important than adherence to grammatical regulations.

You only need two things to do an adequate job: 1) a general awareness of good writing and 2) the ability to find answers. You need the awareness so you can spot potential trouble. It's a matter of having a suspicious mind — of considering every sentence guilty until proven innocent. Finding answers merely requires that you know where to look things up and are willing to do so. (Check the bibliography for our recommendations on reference books.)

Writing guide

Many workgroups can benefit from in-house writing guidelines. These guidelines should give advice on topics such as organization, style, tone, and economy of words.

Although you can find many good books on the subject (we list a few in our bibliography), you can't expect your authors to take the time to read an entire book before every project. Moreover, it can be difficult to apply general advice to specific business-writing problems.

You can save yourself a lot of headaches by condensing the most important rules into a brief guide, complete with real-life examples taken from your own publications. Chapter Seven, "Sample Writing Guide," contains the complete text of the guidelines we use at New Riders Publishing. You should consider building guidelines of your own (or modifying ours).

Grammar and usage guide

A grammar and usage guide is similar to a writing guide, and many companies combine the two. Where a writing guide concentrates on style and technique, a usage guide focuses on rules and consistency. It's purpose is to summarize your house style, so everyone in the company follows the same basic principles.

Don't try to create an exhaustive handbook of English grammar. Limit yourself to the trouble spots, the sticky questions that you and your writers have the most trouble with. Your guide should be no more than a few dozen pages. It will be much more valuable if you illustrate the rules with examples of real-life business prose taken from your own publications.

As you assemble your guide, you may discover problems with many of the standard reference books. First, they often disagree on points of grammar. Second, they often contain so many exceptions that it becomes difficult to condense a simple rule. Third, they aren't always up-to-date.

Obviously, you have to follow the accepted conventions of English usage. The whole point is to make your publications more professional. But since many points are in dispute or transition, don't be afraid to diverge slightly if you feel a rule is impractical or hard to understand. Just be sure to make your changes on the side of simplicity by creating an easy-to-follow general rule and ignoring the arcane exceptions. It's more important to be consistent internally than to be faithful to nineteenth-century practices.

A spelling glossary

Business writing often involves terms not found in the dictionary: product names, proper names, technical jargon, and so on. In addition, good business writing may demand that you deviate from standard spelling. For instance, New Riders publishes many books about software packages. Our books must be consistent with what readers see on the screen — even if the screen is incorrect.

You can make life easier for editors and writers alike if you compile a short spelling glossary. Write down the approved company style for words not in the dictionary. While you're at it, include a few troublesome words that your editors have to correct repeatedly. You may also want to include recommended capitalizations and abbreviations for key terms.

By definition, a spelling glossary will be different for every company. For this reason, we haven't included a full-length sample in this book or on the optional disk. However, Figure 4-1 shows a page from our in-house guide. Perhaps it will give you an idea or two on how to construct one of your own.

> *No passion in the world is equal to the passion to alter someone else's draft.*
>
> H. G. Wells

> | Appendix | Spelling Dictionary |
> |---|---|
> | DOS
   Disk Operating System. | fanfold paper
   Not fan fold paper. |
> | DOS File Ops
   (menu option) | Figure Counter
   (menu option) |
> | dot matrix
   Not dotmatrix. | file format |
> | | File menu |
> | Down-Arrow
   *Note capitalization and
   hyphenation.* | file name
   Not filename |
> | **E** | File Type/Rename
   (menu option) |
> | Edit menu | file type |
> | embed
   Not imbed. | Fill Attributes
   (menu option) |
> | enable | floating-point |
> | End
   The End key. | Footnote Settings
   (menu option) |
> | Enlarged View
   (menu option) | four-column
   Not four column. |
> | Enter
   The Enter key. Not ENTER. | Frame-Wide
   *(dialog box option) Not
   Frame Wide.* |
> | equal sign
   *Not equals sign or equal's
   sign.* | Frame Background
   (menu option) |
> | error-free | Frame menu |
> | Esc
   *The Esc key. Not ESCAPE
   or ESC.* | Frame mode |
> | | Frame Setting
   (menu option) |
> | **F** | Frame Typography
   (menu option) |
> | Facing Pages View
   (menu option) | Full Box |
>
> C-4

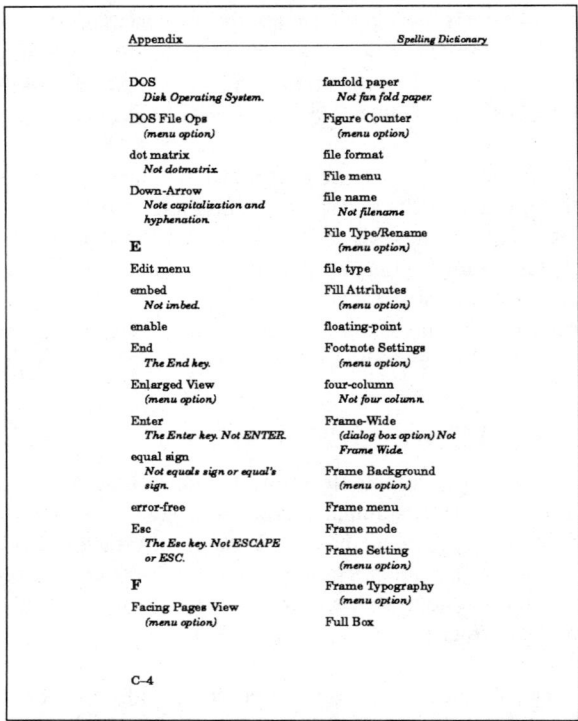

4–1. A sample page from the New Riders spelling glossary.

Style list

So far we've outlined copyediting tools that have a dual role. Writing guides, grammar guides, and spelling glossaries are used both by writers, and by editors. That way everybody is using the same set of blueprints to build their documents.

Now we're going to mention two techniques just for copyeditors: style lists and checklists. Both techniques have been in use by top professionals for many years. We think they can also be helpful in the desktop publishing environment.

A style list is a short reminder of key points — spelling choices, grammar rules, hyphenation decisions, and so on. As you work, you jot down your preferences so you won't have to look them up again (or rely on your memory). Figure 4-2 shows a typical one-page style list. We've filled in a few selections to show you how we use the style list at New Riders.

A style list is an application of the 90-10 rule. Of all the possible style problems, about 10% will cause 90% of your problems. You should record these troublemakers on your style list.

You could make a style list by folding a sheet of paper into 16 squares and labeling each one. But, since you're a desktop publisher, you'll probably want to design one on screen and print it on the laser printer. While you're at it, print out some extra copies for yourself and the others in your workgroup.

In the traditional publishing environment, style lists are more than a reminder for the editor. They are passed on to proofreaders, who use them to confirm that the entire document is internally consistent. If more than one editor works on the same document, you may want to use style lists to pass on key decisions.

(Incidentally, traditional publishers call these documents style *sheets* not style lists. However, so many desktop-publishing programs use style sheets that we started calling them style lists to avoid confusion.)

Copyediting checklists

You can create a checklist for any aspect of editing, from content to consistency to everything in between. A checklist simply keeps you from overlooking an important step. The newer you are and the busier you are, the more helpful checklists become.

We've listed a few ideas to get you started. By necessity, we've created generic starter checklists. You can improve them by 1) adding additional points and 2) substituting specific guidelines for our general comments.

A B	C D	E F file-naming system	G H
I J Instead of: ... Try: ...	K L	M N memory-resident program	O P Q
R S	T U up-to-date	V W	X Y Z
Punctuation Cap complete sentences that follow a colon. terminal commas	Numbers	Abbreviations Acronyms MS-DOS	Typography

4-2. A typical style list. Obviously, each page will be 8.5x11 in. when you make your own.

For instance, where we say "check for errors of fact" a computer book publisher might say "test all tutorial sequences on the computer and confirm that they work exactly as described." Where we say "is the terminology correct and consistent?" a computer publisher might say "have you checked that the book matches the screen word-for-word, letter-for-letter?"

You may also want to consider ways of making checklists part of the work routine. For instance, we often place a checklist at the top of the text file when we start to edit. As we complete each task, we delete it from the list. Some companies put checklists on paper and require editors to sign off on each step to confirm that they've actually done it.

Content

☐ Is the material organized logically?

☐ Is it in the right sequence?

☐ Is the chapter too widely or too narrowly focused?

☐ Has the author left out any major areas?

☐ Has the author included areas that should be deleted (and possibly put into a new, separate document)?

☐ Does it include all the necessary supporting materials (illustrations, tables, footnotes, bibliographies, glossaries)?

☐ Do the introductions and summaries accurately and completely describe the chapters/publication?

☐ Are there errors of fact (dates, quantities, names, assertions)?

☐ Have you received the author's approval for suggested changes?

Good writing is good manners. You can both please and help your public only when you learn how to be the first victim of your writing, how to anticipate a reader's difficulties and to hear yourself as others hear you.

Ritchie R. Ward

Consistency

- ☐ Is the document consistent with company standards (format, typestyles, product names and spellings)?
- ☐ Is the document consistent internally (organization, headings, formats)?
- ☐ Is the terminology correct and consistent?
- ☐ Is the spelling correct and consistent? Have you used the approved spelling checker?

Grammar

- ☐ Does the publication follow the approved reference book?
- ☐ Have you checked the manuscript against the list of common problems in the in-house style guide?
- ☐ Have you listed exceptions and problems on a style list?
- ☐ Have you used the approved grammar checker?

Style

- ☐ Is the material as concise as possible?
- ☐ Is the material written to the correct level? Have you used an approved readability test to find out?
- ☐ Does the material have the correct tone and voice (friendly, neutral, authoritative, etc.)?
- ☐ Are instructions and explanations clear?
- ☐ Do transitions create continuity throughout the document?
- ☐ Have you checked all forward and backward references?

When ideas fail, words come in very handy.
Johann Goethe

Format
☐ Does the format help readers figure out where they are at?

☐ Does the format meet or exceed the level of competing publications?

☐ Are the typestyles and fonts correct?

☐ Do the running heads and other repeating formats match the company standards?

☐ Are illustrations and tables formatted attractively and consistently?

☐ Are illustrations referenced in the text?

☐ Are copyrights and trademarks correctly indicated?

☐ Have you adhered to left/right page restrictions?

Proofreading

Proofreading is the last-chance examination of a manuscript before committing to a final version. Don't confuse it with copyediting. When you copyedit, you must consider the larger issues. Would this material be more appropriate in the previous chapter? Do we need an illustration here? Is there a better way to express this idea? By contrast, when you proofread you look for small things — typos, missing letters, etc.

Sure, there's plenty of overlap. For instance, you should be on the lookout for spelling errors during both copyediting and proofreading. The real differences come in the point of view and the attitude. When you proofread, you look at the details, not the big picture. Proofreading is more mechanical than copyediting. It requires less in the way of intuition and experience, but more in the way of patience and perseverance.

Antonym: the opposite of the word you're trying to think of.

Proofreading tips

Gather the materials you need before you start. If the dictionary's not handy, you might postpone looking up a questionable word — or skip it altogether. Here are a few of the things you may want to have handy:

- in-house grammar and usage guide
- in-house spelling glossary
- dictionary
- thesaurus
- pica ruler for checking spacing and type
- style list compiled by the copy editor (if any)

When you proofread, you must read everything. Everything. Folios, headings, footnotes, captions. Everything. As you will see when you glance through the proofreading checklist below, there's a lot to look out for. Because there are so many details to watch, many proofreaders make repeated passes through a manuscript. How they divide up the work depends on personal working styles. Some people read the headers and footers in one pass, the titles and headings in another, the captions in another, and the text in yet another. Others divide it by problem. First they look for format problems, then they check for spelling, and so on until they've completed everything on the checklist.

As a proofreader, you're not expected to know everything. But you are expected to question everything. If you're not sure what's right, you're expected to know where to look it up.

Part of the proofreader's job may be to compare the final manuscript with the previous version to ensure that all corrections were made, and that new errors haven't crept in. Some people find it easier to make these side-by-side comparisons by using a ruler to go line-by-line.

By all means, proof your own writing, but have someone else read it too. Some professionals claim the best results come from reading the manuscript aloud. (On the other hand, that's not a practical suggestion if you produce 500-page books and work in a crowded office.)

Proofreading marks

By the time you get to the proofreading stage, you should be working on paper. Make sure everyone working on the project uses the same proofreading marks. We highly recommend that you stick to the standard marks in use throughout the industry. Figure 4-3 shows an abbreviated listing that should suffice for most applications. Most grammar, editing, and print-production books contain longer lists.

Proofreading checklist

A proofreading checklist will keep you from overlooking any of the myriad details that amass at the final stages of document production.

This tool is similar to the copyediting checklist mentioned earlier, except that it tends to be longer and more detailed. We have included a sample below, which you can modify to fit your own situation. As always, the more you customize the checklist, the more valuable it becomes. Be prepared to revise it as often as necessary to keep it up-to-date.

Overall format
☐ margins

☐ widows and orphans

☐ spacing between elements

☐ ruling lines

☐ fonts

Headers and footers
☐ pagination

☐ format (type size, font, spacing, ruling lines)

☐ spelling

☐ content

Symbol	Example	Meaning
∧	sample ˆtext (t inserted)	insert
ℓ	sample text⸝	delete
◡	samp l͡e text	close up
⌐	⌐sample text	move left
⌐ (reversed)	sample text⌐	move right
∾	sample t(xe)t	transpose
¶	sample text ¶ More...	paragraph
#	sample#text	blank character
≡	s̲a̲m̲ple t̲e̲xt	capitalize
=	s̲ample t̲ext	small caps
≡ (triple underline)	sample text	all caps
/	S̸ample T̸ext	make lowercase
stet....	sample t̶e̶x̶t̶ stet	leave as it was
#>	#> sample text	line space (below)
⌐⌐	⌐sample text⌐	center
sp (circled)	(s.t.) — sp	spell out
——	sample text	set in italic type
∽∽	sample text (wavy underline)	set in boldface type
Rom (circled)	(sample text) Rom	set in roman type
—ǀ—m	sample∧text (m inserted)	insert em dash
—ǀ—n	sample∧text (n inserted)	insert en dash
⊙	sample text⊙	insert period
∧	sample text∧	insert comma
∨	sample text∨	insert apostrophe

4–3. Use these standard proofreading marks to note corrections on printed manuscripts.

Titles and headings
☐ spelling

☐ capitalization

☐ format (type size, font, spacing, ruling lines)

☐ construction

Words
☐ hyphenation

☐ spelling

☐ capitalization

☐ abbreviations and acronyms

☐ proper names

☐ product names

☐ trademarks and copyrights

☐ use of bold and italic

Sentences
☐ punctuation

☐ widows and orphans

☐ capitalization in clauses

Tables
☐ consistent format

☐ headings/captions/labels

☐ text references

> *I believe more in the scissors than I do in the pencil.*
> Truman Capote

Numbers
☐ correct quantity

☐ correct format

☐ dates

☐ use of numerals

☐ hierarchal style

☐ consecutive numbering

Pictures
☐ picture placement, size, position, alignment, spacing, and accuracy

☐ text references

☐ figure numbers

☐ captions

☐ callouts

Other
☐ check TOC for accuracy

☐ spot check index for accuracy

Indexing

Those of you who work on long documents may become involved in indexing. Whether you actually prepare the index, or are just responsible for checking it, keep the principles explained below in mind.

How you prepare the index depends on your preferences and the capabilities of your software. Decide in advance who will be responsible for the first draft and how it will be done.

The traditional method is to use index cards (that's why they call them *index* cards). You list one topic per card. As you find new page locations for that topic, you note them on the card in sequence. When you've finished the manuscript, you type and format the index.

Some word-processing and desktop-publishing programs have indexing capabilities. If you wish to index electronically, be sure to coordinate with everyone concerned. Don't let authors waste time indexing in the word processor if your page-layout program can't use the information. For instance, you can enter index marks in a word processor for importation into Xerox Ventura Publisher — but you must enter them with codes Ventura can recognize. Ventura cannot accept indexing performed with a word processor's native commands.

When you use index cards, it's easy to look back to see what you called a similar topic or how you spelled the entry ("did I say *rules*? Or was it *ruling line*?") When you index electronically, you don't have that luxury. You quickly lose track of names and cross references, especially when working on long documents.

One solution is to write the topics down on paper as you go along. At New Riders, we do it another way. When we index the first chapter electronically, we print out the result. This printout becomes our guide and reminder sheet for the chapter two. When we've finished with chapter two, we print out a combined index for both chapters. The combined printout is our guide for chapter three. We continue in this fashion chapter by chapter.

However you prepare the index, *be sure to proofread it*. An index is worse than useless if the page numbers aren't accurate. Don't assume that it's correct just because the computer did the work.

For example, some publishers add extra pages to the end of their chapters. These pages don't appear in the printed version. They are used to record an edit history, to hold templates for pictures, and so on. If you forget to delete these pages before generating the index, you will throw off the computer's numbering.

What to include in an index

Indexing is more art than science. The trick is to guess every different way a novice might look for a topic, then include an index entry for each one.

As a starting point, make sure that every word in the glossary is included. In addition, most main headings will contain words or topics that should be indexed. On the other hand, you should index only significant information. You don't have time to include every single place the word "text" is printed in the manuscript. You do, however, want to list every spot where the reader can find something important about the concept of text.

Main entries

There are usually several ways to refer to a topic. As the main entry, choose the one you think readers will use most often.

Consistency is essential in any index, but even more so if you are indexing electronically. The computer is not smart enough to know that you meant the same thing when you used the words "edit," "edits," "editing," and "text editing." It will create separate entries for all four. As a general rule, choose the singular form of a word. Use the plural only if that is the normal way readers refer to a topic.

It can be difficult to remember how you indexed a topic earlier. Make a list by hand or generate one from the computer and keep it by your side as you work.

Secondary entries

When in doubt, subdivide. If you think a topic will come up more than three times, create secondary entries:

    Frames
        Adding 32, 44, 188
        Definition 29
        Deleting 35
        Line around 63, 122

See entries
After you have chosen the main entry, think of every way a reasonable person might refer to the topic. Then cross-reference the other possibilities with "See" entries.
    Containers
        See Frames

It only takes a moment to enter a few extra cross-references. Those cross-references can save a frustrated user hours of time. As you are dreaming up cross-references, don't forget to invert phrases where necessary. For instance, suppose the main entry is "Underlying Page." You should also cross-reference the inverted version:
    Page, Underlying
        See Underlying Page

See Also entries
As you are indexing, you may encounter topics that are closely related to others. If you think the reader would benefit from reading the other entry, create a See Also reference:
    Frames
        Adding 32, 44, 188
        Definition 29
        Deleting 35
        Line around 63, 122
        See Also Underlying Page

An editor's tool kit

This chapter has focused on tools that help editors. We've listed these tools below, along a few other items that you may want to consider. We also show the chapter(s) in this book where each item is discussed. As with all our recommendations, the idea is to pick and choose from the possibilities to build a customized tool kit for your company.

- Writing guide
  Chapter Four, Chapter Seven

- Grammar and usage guide
  Chapter Four, Chapter Six

- Spelling and capitalization glossary
  Chapter Four, Chapter Six

- Style list
  Chapter Four

- Copyediting and proofreading checklists
  Chapter Four

- List of proofreading marks
  Chapter Four

- File-naming and file-location guidelines (if the editor is responsible for creating or modifying any electronic files)
  Chapter Two, Chapter Three

- Formatting guidelines (if the editor is responsible for checking format specs as well)
  Chapter Two, Chapter Five

- Reference books
  Chapter Ten

- Software (spell checkers, grammar/style checkers, electronic thesaurus)

- Pica ruler

Formatting pages 5

So far we've shown you how to set up your organization for desktop publishing, create pictures, and write and edit documents. But it's not until the formatting (page-layout) stage that you discover whether your methods really work. Formatting is where everything comes together — where you take the text, the pictures, and the editing done earlier and merge them into a final document.

This chapter does not discuss the specifics of any page-layout program, nor does it delve into graphic design. As with the rest of this book, it focuses on efficiency tips — nuts-and-bolts techniques you can put to work no matter which software you use.

We've organized our tips sequentially by task. While there's no standard way of laying out pages, the following workflow is fairly typical:

- Organizing the project
- File conversion and cleanup
- Page layout
- Job tracking
- Archiving

Organizing the project

We've discussed organization tips previously. We'll touch on them briefly again here, this time from the perspective of the layout operator.

Organization is more important for the layout operator than for anyone else on the DTP team. Everything flows through the layout workstation sooner or later. If it bogs down, it clogs the entire operation.

Why should you waste time searching for files and chasing down pictures? A simple organizational scheme enables you to put your finger on everything you need in an instant. Remember these key points:

1. Use a standard file-naming system, such as the system explained in Chapters Two and Three.
2. Organize the hard disk logically, as explained in Chapter Two. Use the same basic system for every project.
3. Set up a paper-filing system to supplement your electronic controls.

A standardized system for paper files can go a long way towards streamlining operations. If you do short documents, you may be able to get by with a single file per project. Longer documents require more subdivision. Whatever you settle on, use the same system for every project. By way of illustration, the following list shows the file system in use by one of our New Riders production offices:

Administration
    Outlines
    Checklists
    Correspondence
    Permission letters

Editorial
    (One file for each chapter, including separate files for front matter, appendixes, and indexes. Artwork goes in corresponding chapter file.)
    Chapter 01
    Chapter 02
    etc.

Marketing
    Author questionnaire
    Sales materials
    Press releases
    Reviews and testimonials

We're not suggesting that these are the right categories for your documents. The point is that we use the same setup for every book. Editors and layout operators can switch between projects with a minimum of relearning time. A standard filing system might benefit your operation, too, even if you work by yourself.

At New Riders, we use these same files for our backup disks. At the end of each day, the layout operators back up their work. They put the backup disks for each chapter in the paper file for that chapter.

The next morning, they pull out the disk for the chapter they want to work on. If someone else wants to work on the same chapter, he looks in the file for the disk. If it's missing, he knows someone else is working on it. We set up this procedure to avoid accidental duplication, where two people work on different versions of the same file and cancel out each other's changes.

File conversion and cleanup

You'll get most of your text and pictures via electronic files. That sounds fast and convenient. In reality, you may need to clean up and/or convert those files before you can use them.

Filing cabinet: where papers get lost alphabetically.

Try to automate conversion and cleanup with macros. If you're forced to do things manually, set up a checklist so you don't have to rely on your memory each time you start a new document. Consider batching your work, so you convert all the files at once.

Converting word-processing files

You may have to transfer word-processing files from one hardware platform to another, via telecommunications, network transfer, or disk swapping. Once you have the files on the right machine, you'll have to convert them to a file format the page-layout program will recognize.

If the author followed the suggestions in Chapter Two, "Creating Text," the file should be fairly clean. If not, you'll have to strip out the extraneous garbage that would otherwise clog up the page-layout program.

In some cases, you can set up the transfer or telecommunications program to strip out unwanted characters. Sometimes, the page-layout program will convert them. In other cases, you can search and replace with your word processor. Or, if the worst happens, you may have to scan the file on the screen and make the changes manually. Before loading a word-processing file, make sure that you've taken care of these potential problems one way or another:

1. Deletion of unwanted carriage returns.

2. Deletion of unwanted tab stops.

3. Deletion of extra spaces after punctuation.

4. Conversion of spaces to tab stops in tables.

5. Conversion of double hyphens to em dashes.

6. Conversion of inch marks to open and close quotes.

7. Conversion of typewriter characters to their true typesetting equivalents (bullets, ellipses, trademark symbols, copyright symbols, etc.).

Ideally, you should set up a single macro to perform a series of search and replace operations. If that's not possible, write a short checklist, so operators won't forget which steps to take.

Converting picture files

You may also need to convert picture files. In some cases, the only way to get a graphic into the page-layout program is to convert it to a different format. Don't forget that there may be different versions of a format. Be sure you're converting to the right one.

Even page-layout programs that claim to support numerous graphics formats have their favorites. For example, Xerox Ventura Publisher is able to work with some graphic files directly. Others must be converted. When it converts, Ventura keeps both the original and the converted version. The required disk space is effectively doubled. The longer the document, the more significant this extra space becomes.

What's more, page-layout programs often claim to accept a graphic format when they really only accept certain graphic elements. The page-layout program may bring in the lines, but reject the fill patterns. Sometimes you can get around these limitations by converting the picture to a different format before you load it into the page-layout program.

Experiment with graphics files until you find the best formats for your type of work. Then record your findings so you don't have to reinvent the wheel for the next document.

Page layout

Once you've gathered and organized your materials, you're ready to put together the pages. Here are a few efficiency tips that have worked for other desktop publishers.

Preformatting

Experienced desktop publishers say that preformatting provides major cost and time benefits.

> *Change can nickel and dime you to death.*

We've already discussed specific preformatting techniques in Chapter Two, "Creating Text," and Chapter Four, "Editing." In this section, we just want to remind layout operators that they can make their lives easier by encouraging editors, writers, and illustrators to preformat.

Preformatting doesn't have to take extra time. Just make sure that authors and editors are working in a compatible word processor. Then ensure that they are using fonts, styles, or tags you can import.

You're more likely to get cooperation if you provide authors and editors with tools that make it easier to preformat. Depending on the software you use, you should be able to take advantage of preformatting aides like these:

- tag lists and tag dictionaries (see Chapter 8 for an example)
- formatting samples
- word-processing templates
- predefined macros for word processors
- typing guidelines

Format standards

For maximum efficiency, it's essential to create and record formatting standards. You don't want to rewrite formatting rules each time; nor do you want discrepancies within your documents; nor can you afford to start over again because of format changes. We speak from experience. We discovered the hard way at New Riders how costly it can be to change horses in midstream (or, in our case, style sheets in mid-project).

The first step is to arrive at standards. Desktop publishing allows changes at any point in the production process. This flexibility is one of its greatest strengths. It's also one of the biggest drawbacks. Unless you're careful, you can waste hours or even days fiddling with the page design. Small changes often have big repercussions when they ripple through a long manuscript. Changing the body text by a single point, for instance, could mean laying out an entire book over again to get pictures to appear on the correct pages.

Format standards

In theory, the best solution is to not to change your page design after you've started. But real life doesn't work that way. As you get into a document, you often come up against unexpected problems that force changes. Still, you should make it your business to lock down the format as soon as possible. Resist any alterations that aren't essential.

Once you arrive at a form, you need to record it. Your documentation might be something as simple as handwritten notes on a thumbnail sketch. Most companies, however, will want to document their designs more thoroughly. Some page-layout programs, for instance, permit you to print out a listing of the key settings and attributes (Figure 5-1).

5–1. Some desktop publishers document their page designs on paper.

Likewise, tag dictionaries like the sample in Chapter Eight are a way to record a format on paper. Even if your program doesn't use style sheets, you can still create a document that illustrates each of the key page elements. A design dictionary makes it much easier for the other people on your team to understand and work with your format.

Paper documentation is a good idea, and an easy way to distribute your designs to others. But the best way to record your format standards is via electronic templates.

Templates and style sheets

Templates serve several important functions. First, they preserve the talent of an expert designer in a form non-designers can use. Second, they enforce consistency — if everybody starts from the same template, the documents will look the same. Third, they save time.

Every page-layout program has some method of creating reusable document templates. Usually, you work on a document until it looks just right. Then you empty it of text and graphics, leaving only repeating elements and formats (Figure 5-2). Often you leave *placeholders* to identify what goes where: "This is a main heading" or "table of contents here." The next user deletes the placeholders and substitutes real text and graphics.

Most templates include these ingredients:

- margins
- columns
- headers and footers
- page numbering
- logos
- formats for standard text elements — titles, headings, main text, lists, tables, captions
- formats for pictures — sizes, captions, etc.

5–2. A template is a document that is empty of everything except formatting instructions and repeating page elements. To use it, you fill it in with new text and graphics.

The more page elements you define in advance, the more useful the template. Ideally, you will include every eventuality, so users never have to create any elements from scratch. They can concentrate strictly on layout. For instance, consider the idea of building formats for a variety of picture sizes and styles. Even though you won't need every size for every document, it's nice to have them on hand when you do. You can use the ones you need and delete the rest before printing the document.

> *The road to ignorance is paved with good editions.*
> G. B. Shaw

Style/Template libraries

If you always work on the same kind of document, you may only need one or two templates. But people who produce different kinds of documents will want to take the template concept one step further. They will want to build a library of designs.

A template library boosts productivity. It puts a variety of designs at your fingertips. It can have other benefits, too. If the templates follow the same design approach, they can achieve an attractive, recognizable look for everything your company distributes to the public. Major corporations spend hundreds of thousands of dollars to establish and enforce corporate identify programs. You can achieve the same benefits by spending a few days building and distributing a template library.

On the other hand, a template library can be more work than it is worth if you don't organize it effectively. Be sure to follow some type of file-naming and file-location system so formats are easy to find. In addition, you'd be wise to create a notebook of approved formats for easy reference. If you prefer, you can print them out in thumbnail format (Figure 5-3).

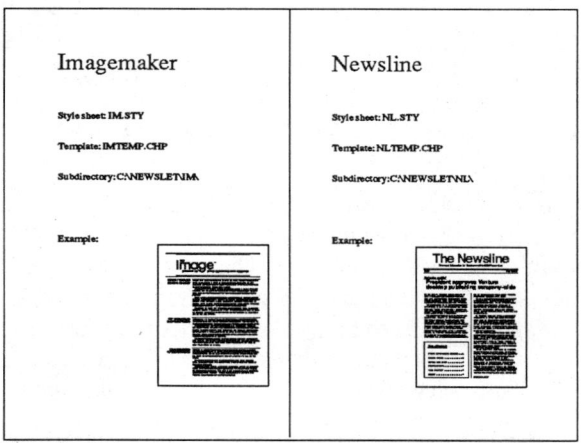

5-3. Consider documenting your template library with thumbnail printouts in a notebook.

You may also need to take steps to make sure that unskilled users don't modify and damage the designs. Some companies have a *designated designer*. Anyone can use a format or suggest changes. But only the designated designer is allowed to alter the designs, so they remain appropriate and consistent. Or, depending on your system, you may be able to lock the designs electronically, so they can be used but not modified.

Finally, you'll want to make sure you have a master copy of the template library secured in a safe location, where no one can accidentally write over all your hard work. And don't forget to include instructions with each copy, to remind users to save the document under a new name as soon as they open the template.

If you're thinking that creating a template library sounds like a lot of work, keep in mind that you don't have to build it from scratch. Almost all page-layout programs come with a starter set of designs. You may also be able to buy additional designs from the software manufacturer, or from outside companies.

Picture techniques

Illustrations are an important part of most desktop-published documents. Here is an assortment of tips to save you time and give your illustrations more impact.

Text references

Marketing materials don't require text references. On the other hand, books and technical documents will usually benefit from a phrase in the text that identifies the illustration. "See Figure 1" is a typical example.

If you use a text reference, try to place the picture as close to it as possible. However, *do not put the picture before the reference*. A picture that mysteriously appears on the page with no reference confuses readers. Then, when they do get to the reference, they have to stop and turn back. This common sense rule sounds obvious. Yet it is surprising how many otherwise good books lose some of their effectiveness through poor picture placement.

Keep pictures separate

Keep images separate from the text as long as possible. Don't combine them into a page layout until you have determined which pictures are definitely going to stay in the manuscript, and just where they belong. Review Chapter Three, "Creating Pictures," for suggestions on working with a separate picture printout prior to page layout.

Art log

If illustrations are a major stumbling block for your group, you may want to consider a technique long in use by book publishers. They create an *art log* for every project.

This log records the essential information for every picture. Modified for desktop publishing, it might list the following:

- figure number
- page number of text reference
- file name
- file format
- caption
- type of illustration (line art, photo, etc.)
- brief description
- source (if permissions are required)

With today's desktop-publishing technology, it would be very easy to combine the information with a thumbnail printout of the picture itself. Or you could combine the art log with the picture printout described in Chapter Three.

Publishing is a dog-eat-dog world, so sharpen your clauses.

Page-layout tips

Use a checklist
Create a task checklist to automate some of the layout process for you. That way, you won't need to worry about remembering tedious chores like resetting the page counter. We've listed some tasks you may want to include below:

☐ Save the template under a new file name.

☐ Load text files.

☐ Load picture file(s).

☐ Reset the page/chapter/figure/table counters.

☐ Set the headers.

☐ Set the footers.

☐ Insert index markers.

☐ Check for widows and orphans.

☐ Check for bad page breaks.

☐ Save frequently.

☐ Back up the document each time you work on it.

☐ Complete the footnotes.

Do the layout last
Discourage the team from embarking on page layout too soon. Inevitably, both text and pictures will require changes. When that happens, you'll have to redo the page layout. Again.

In the old days, writers, editors, and illustrators were careful to get things right *before* the manuscript was typeset and laid out. Guess what — that's still good advice today. True, you don't have to call up a typesetter and a paste-up artist to make changes anymore. Now you can make them right on your desktop. But just because you won't receive a bill doesn't mean the changes are free.

To save time and effort, devise a system whereby documents only go through layout once.

Divide long projects

Divide long projects logically into small segments. Smaller files are easier to work on and less prone to computer crashes and software disasters. Shorter files are also easier to share, and to back up onto floppy disks.

Distribute disk labels

If you're tired of deciphering tiny, illegible disk labels with cryptic notes, consider distributing standard disk labels to all your authors, editors, and illustrators, and layout operators. Local stationery stores carry labels for laser printers. Design a format you like and print as many sheets as you need. Include boxes for checking off essential information, and spaces for dates and file names (Figure 5-4).

```
Initials: _____    Project: _____    Date: ___/___/___
Format: ❑ 360 ❑ 1.2    Copy method: ❑ DOS ❑ Multi-Chapter
Files: _____    _____    _____
       _____    _____    _____
       _____    _____    _____

🚲 New Riders Publishing
```

5-4. Even something as obvious as standard disk labels can simplify workgroup publishing.

Job tracking

Since everything flows through the page-layout workstation, the operator is likely to get stuck with job tracking — the task of recording progress. Actually, job tracking is more than just reporting whether or not things are behind schedule. It is also the function which ensures that all the details necessary to complete a publication are attended to. The forms and checklists used to keep track of progress also serve as reminders so nothing gets overlooked.

Job tracking doesn't have to be complex. You can type out a list and cross things off. If you work in a group, you can keep an edit history at the end of the text file (Figure 5-5).

```
2/10/89 JB First draft revision
for Managing DTP. Gave to BR
for illustrations and editing.

2/14/89 BR Format, edit first
draft

2/15 BR BR Edit revised draft,
create and insert illustra-
tions. To JB for approval

2/16/89 JB Review formatted
chapter. Gave to BR for minor
revisions.

2/17/89 BR Minor revisions,
print final copy

2/21/89  BR Changed page mar-
gins. Reformat and reprint.
```

5–5. Job tracking doesn't have to be fancy. You may be able to get by with a few notes at the end of the file.

For examples of paper-based job tracking, see Chapter Nine, "Sample Checklists."

> *The last thing that we find in making a book is to know what we must put first.*
> Blaise Pascal

Archiving

Since the dawn of computers, books and magazines have been admonishing users to back up religiously. We'll assume you already know the standard litany of warnings and horror stories, and confine ourselves to adding one new one: revision.

For some reason, desktop publishers rarely think about revisions. Maybe it's the exhilaration of finishing a project. Or maybe it's our subconscious minds rebelling at the thought of going through it all over again.

Consequently, we sometimes wake up six months or a year later to discover we can't find all the files we need to reconstruct a document; or we've lost the photographs that went with it; or the floppy disk with the only copy has been damaged; and so on.

What you need is a simple system the whole office can use — one that backs up projects as you go along, so you can never lose more than a few hours work. We'll explain our simple system as an example.

The basis of the New Riders system is one file folder for each chapter. Into that folder goes the latest printout, and the latest floppy disk backup. Layout operators update the floppy disk at the end of every work session, so the backups are always current.

When we've finished the project, those interim floppy disks stay in the file folders as our final backup. Then we make a second, separate set of disks. These safety copies are stored off-site.

On top of our project archives, we also back up the hard disk(s) on every computer each Friday. Once a month, we rotate the current backup disks or tapes to off-site storage sites.

Our system isn't anything fancy. But it's worth telling you about because we have an organized method and we stick to it. You should too.

A formatting tool kit

The list below includes some of the tools you can use to simplify page layout. It also shows the chapter(s) in this book where each item is discussed.

- Conversion/cleanup checklist for word-processing files
  Chapter Four, Chapter Seven

- File-naming and file-location guidelines
  Chapter Two, Chapter Three

- Formatting guidelines or standards
  Chapter Two, Chapter Five

- Layout Checklist
  Chapter Five

- Art log
  Chapter Five

- List of proofreading marks
  Chapter Four

- Tag lists and dictionaries
  Chapter Two, Chapter Four, Chapter Five, Chapter Eight

- Document templates
  Chapter Five

- Picture templates
  Chapter Five

- Disk labels
  Chapter Five

- Production Checklists
  Chapter Nine

- Pica ruler

Reference

Part Two

Sample Grammar and Usage Guide 6

It's counterproductive to stop the flow of writing or editing to search through style manuals and dictionaries. *The Chicago Manual of Style*, for instance, is 700 pages long. Most companies will benefit, therefore, from an abbreviated version — a few dozen pages that explain the most common trouble spots.

WARNING: We don't consider this sample guide to be the final word on correct English usage.

Although we used the standard references when compiling this guide, we did not hesitate to deviate from the traditional rules if necessary. Since we produce computer books, the need to stay consistent with the software overrides the need to stay consistent with English grammar. In other words, some software packages break the rules of grammar. We occasionally choose to follow their (admittedly bad) example so our books will match what users encounter in the program.

We certainly do not intend this guide as a replacement for *The Chicago Manual of Style,* Strunk and White's *Elements of Style*, or any of the other classics. But even though you should not use it as the final authority on grammar, you can refer to it as a useful listing of key topics. The areas we have included are the ones that give the most trouble to our authors and editors. We suspect that many of them will apply to your situation as well.

Building a usage guide

One quick, easy way to build your own guide is to use our list of topics as a starting point. Delete the subjects that don't apply. Add new ones that are especially important to your company. Then review each section to make sure it reflects the way you like to do things. Whenever possible, substitute examples taken from your own publications. If you have purchased the optional Managing disk, you already have the text file. (You also have the chapter files and style sheet if you want to use Xerox Ventura Publisher to do the formatting.)

To be effective, an in-house grammar and usage guide must be *short* and *specific*. Keeping it short presents the greatest challenge. English has so many rules, and so many exceptions, that it becomes difficult to boil them down into a useful summary. At New Riders, our solution was to include only the general rule and to leave out most of the esoteric exceptions. We recommend that you resist the temptation to cover every situation. If an in-house guide goes much beyond 25 pages, you'll have a hard time convincing authors and editors to scan it before they start to work.

The job of keeping the usage guide to a manageable size will be easier if you concentrate on the second goal: keeping it specific. Try to eliminate topics and problems that don't crop up very often in your documents. As mentioned above, you should also use examples from your company's publications. Our guide, for instance, uses phrases and situations taken directly from our computer books.

A spelling and capitalization guide may also be useful to your writers and editors. Here you can address words that are commonly misspelled by your authors, as well as terms that pertain specifically to your business. We haven't included a sample guide here, because each company's needs will vary widely. Chapter Four, "Editing," shows a sample page from ours.

The balance of this chapter duplicates the in-house grammar and usage guide for New Riders Publishing. You will note that it occasionally refers to specific procedures for Xerox Ventura Publisher, the desktop-publishing software we use to format our books.

Usage Rules

This usage guide lists several dozen grammatical danger zones. These are the topics that most often trip up authors and editors. If you don't know how to handle a situation, look here to find our suggestion.

Although grammar may not seem like an important issue, we view it as critical. If you can train yourself in a few basic areas, you will improve your publications. Bad or inconsistent grammar detracts from your credibility with readers. It also means that your editors must spend valuable time chasing down minor mistakes.

It doesn't take any longer to do it right. For instance, it doesn't take any longer to type periods *inside* quotation marks and *outside* parentheses. Let me qualify that: It doesn't take any longer once you know the proper rule. It will, however, make things harder if you have to look it up each time.

To avoid repeated trips to this guide, we suggest a technique used by professional editors: a *style list*. As you encounter questions about spelling and style, you write the answers on the style list so you won't have to look them up again. In Chapter 4, "Editing," we've included a sample style list and instructions on how to make your own.

If you cannot find an answer to a question, please make a note of it for your editor. If you have a suggestion, jot it down right on the page, and send us a photocopy. You can also refer to *The Chicago Manual of Style* as a backup. We use it ourselves. Please note, however, that if there is a conflict between this guide and *Chicago*, we want you to use our suggestions. They have been geared to computer books.

Abbreviations

Minimize abbreviations. For instance, do not use the abbreviations *e.g.* and *i.e.* Instead, spell out the words *for example* and *that is.*

Acronyms

Minimize acronyms, except those that have achieved universal status, such as RAM. Use all caps for acronyms. Always spell them out (in parentheses) the first time you use them, even the common ones:
    First determine the available RAM (Random Access Memory)...

Addressing an editor

Always agree with an editor. Follow your affirmation with an honorific:
    Jawohl, Herr Editor!

You may append a comment after the honorific:
    Indeed, Your Truculence, your marginal notes were most inspiring.

Affect, effect

Affect as a verb means to influence. Avoid using it as a noun:
    Correct:
        Choosing Set Font will not affect the rest of the paragraph.

Effect as a noun means result. Avoid using it as a verb:
    Correct:
        This command may have a surprising effect.

Although, while

Use *although* to indicate contrast. If you can substitute the phrase *even though*, you can safely use although:
    Correct:
        Although Ventura is difficult at first, it repays your learning efforts with power and convenience.

Use *while* to indicate time. If you can substitute the phrase *at the same time that*, use while:
   Correct:
      While you are still holding down the button, drag the mouse...

Apostrophes

Apostrophes indicate possession, not the plural.

The possessive of singular nouns is formed by an apostrophe and an *s*:
   To use Ventura's indexing features, you must first...

The possessive of plural nouns that end with *s* is formed with an apostrophe only:
   Check the tags' attributes...

Exception: Use an apostrophe to indicate the plural if the use of an *s* alone would cause confusion:
   Wrong:
      Change all the *bs* to *ps*.
   Correct:
      Change all the *b*'s to *p*'s.

Boldface

Do not use boldface to emphasis words within a sentence. Use italics.

Can, may

Use *can* to express ability or power. Use *may* to express permission.

Capitalization

All caps or *upper case* means to capitalize every letter of every word:
   HERE IS A SENTENCE IN ALL CAPS.

Use all caps for acronyms, company names like IBM, file names, and subdirectory names. Do not use all caps for emphasis within a sentence — use italics. Do not type titles, headings, or subheadings in all caps.

Initial caps means to capitalize the first letter of every word (except for prepositions and conjunctions, which are not capitalized):
    Here Is a Sentence in Initial Caps.

Upper and lower or *down style* means to capitalize only the first letter of the sentence or phrase (and proper nouns):
    Here is a sentence in upper and lower.

Lower case means you should not capitalize anything:
    here is a phrase in lower case

Here are the capitalization rules we have settled on at New Riders, listed by category:

Chapter numbers
Use initial caps when referring to another chapter in your own book. Spell out the number:
    In Chapter Three, "Blowing Your Own Horn," you learned how to...

Computer acronyms
Use all caps:
    At the DOS prompt...
    The ASCII file format...
    A minimum of 512K RAM...

Exception: KHz

Dialog boxes
Do not capitalize the words *dialog box*:
    The Ruling Line Above dialog box...
    Choose OK to close the dialog box...

Dialog box options
Capitalize the same way the program capitalizes.

File and subdirectory names
Use all caps:
    C:\POWER\ SAMPLE.CHP
    Load the file 8DESIGN.TXT from the C:\TEMP subdirectory.

Headings
All headings, regardless of their level, should use upper and lower (down style). Only the chapter title has initial caps:
    Chapter numbers
    Computer acronyms
    Dialog box options

Exception: Capitalize proper names in headings:
    Dialog boxes for Ventura Publisher

Hyphenated compounds
In headings and titles: If you capitalize the first word, capitalize the second one too:
    High-Resolution graphics

Menus
Capitalize the name, but not the word *menu*:
    File menu
    Edit menu

Menu options
Use upper and lower:
    Select Load Diff. Style from the File menu.
    Select Remove Text/File from the Edit menu.

Notes
Put the first word of notes, warnings, and tips in all caps:
    NOTE: Most of the sample text files have...

Parts of the book
Use lower case if you are referring to a generic concept:
    The appendixes include additional helpful material...

Use initial caps if you are referring to a chapter in your own book:
> For more details see Appendix A, "The Tag List."

Use upper and lower if you are referring to any other specific part of your own book:
> In the previous section, Menu options...

Captions

Most illustrations require a label or description. Write them as complete sentences that can stand alone. (Some readers skim captions without reading the accompanying text.)

Colons

A colon introduces an example or amplification, a list, or a series. Place colons outside quotation marks.

Introducing an example

A colon often takes the place of an implied *namely*. Do not capitalize the phrase that follows the colon unless it is a complete sentence:
> In Chapter Two you will learn three critical concepts: design, pagination, and page layout.

Use a colon to introduce an example if it follows the sentence directly. Likewise, use a colon to introduce a sample screen or sample page. This usage guide uses colons in this manner.

Introducing a list

The terms *as follows* and *the following* require a colon if followed directly by the list:
> The steps are as follows:
> 1. Press the mouse button.
> 2. Drag the cursor to the right...

Introducing a series

You can use a colon to introduce a series at the end of a sentence. However, if you use expressions such as *namely, for instance, for ex-*

ample, or *that is,* do not use a colon unless the series consists of grammatically complete clauses:
> You can draw a variety of graphic shapes in Ventura, for example, lines, rectangles, and circles.
> For example: Sara used WordStar for the text; Anthony used Adobe Illustrator for the pictures; and Edward used Ventura for layout.

Commas

The use of the comma is mostly a matter of good judgment; use it if it make the sentence easier to read. Here are a few guidelines.

Comparisons
Separate comparisons and contrasts with commas:
> The faster the circuit, the more heat it generates.

Coordinate adjectives
Separate coordinate adjectives (two adjectives that modify the same noun) with commas:
> The sharp, colorful display...

If you can substitute the word *and*, use the comma. If you cannot substitute *and,* use a hyphen:
> The high-performance, IBM-compatible display...

Serial commas
These days, writers and editors often omit the comma at the end of a series. However, many technical publishers still retain the so-called terminal comma, because it helps avoid confusion. We prefer that you use it in New Riders manuscripts:
> Proceed to pages 33, 34, and 35.

Commas and dependent clauses
Use a comma to separate a dependent clause that precedes the main clause:
> Once you have generated the file, you can...

We prefer that you follow this rule even for short introductory phrases:
> In addition, you must consider several other...

However, many writers prefer...

Commas and quotation marks
Place commas *inside* quotation marks:
> Select the paragraphs "XYZ Corporation," "Research," and "Planning."

Commas and parentheses
Place commas *outside* parentheses:
> Although you can draw freehand (if you have a steady hand), it's best to use the snap-to grid feature for accuracy.

Contractions

As a general rule, do not use contractions. This rule is especially important in titles, headings or subheadings, and in step-by-step instructions, where contractions can make a sentence harder to read and understand:
> Instead of:
>> You'll discover many features in Ventura's menus:
>
> Try:
>> You will discover many features in Ventura's menus.

Exception: Contractions are appropriate in introductory sections and books that are not highly technical (like this handbook, for instance). They establish a down-to-earth, friendly tone:
> That's all there is to it.
> Don't be concerned. You'll have plenty of chances to...

If you have trouble remembering when you should and should not use contractions, leave them out altogether.

E.g.

Use *for example* instead.

Ellipses

Use an ellipsis (...) to indicate missing material and incomplete sentences:
> However, many writers prefer...

You may use other punctuation on either side of the three ellipsis dots. For instance, use a period after an ellipsis at the end of a sentence.

Typing the ellipsis in the text file
Do not type three periods for the ellipsis. Instead, insert the Ventura bracket code for the true typographic ellipsis character (<193>). Do not type spaces before or after the bracket code. For instance, here is how a previous example looks in the text file:
```
However, many writers prefer<193>
```

Em dash
Typewriters have only the hyphen. Typesetting systems, by contrast, have a hyphen plus two dashes of differing lengths:
Em dash: —
En dash: –
Hyphen: -

Think of the em dash as a powerful comma. It is one of several alternatives for setting off parenthetical expressions and appositives. You can also use it as a sentence interrupter:
Use the em dash — not the hyphen — to set off parenthetical expressions.
Use the em dash to set off an appositive — a restatement of a noun in different terms.
Use the em dash as a sentence interrupter for emphasis — like this.

See also *Parenthetical expressions* for guidelines on using the em dash.

Typing the em dash in the text file
Use two hyphens to represent the em dash. Put a space before and after the two hyphens. Ventura will convert the hyphens to an em dash when it loads the file.
In your word processor:
```
Use the em dash for emphasis -- like this.
```
In Ventura:
Use the em dash for emphasis — like this.

En dash

Use the en dash to indicate continuing, inclusive numbers such as dates, time, or reference numbers:
```
...during the period 1987-1989
...pages 45-48.
```

Do not type a hyphen in the text file to indicate an en dash. Use the Ventura bracket code (<196>) instead:
```
...during the period 1987<196>1989
...pages 45<196>48.
```

Ensure

Use *ensure* to mean guarantee. Use *insure* only for references to insurance.

Exclamation marks

Don't use them! Please! They signal an immature writing style!

File names

Type file names in all caps:
   Load the text file SAMPLE.TXT.

Fractions

See *Numbers*.

Hyphens

Use hyphens only for hyphenated words, not in place of en dashes (see En dashes above). Use two consecutive hyphens with a space on each side in place of an em dash (see Em dashes above).

Hyphenating compound adjectives

When two or more words are combined to form an adjective, the result is a *compound adjective*. The component words may be other parts of

speech, but when combined they serve to modify a noun. Hyphenate compound adjectives if they appear *before* the noun:
> A two-column layout...
> Use the snap-to grid to...
> A 12-year-old boy...
> An up-to-the-minute page design is not always...

Do not, however, hyphenate two words if the first is an adverb modifying the second adjective. (Most adverbs end in *-ly*.)
> completely known material
> very high frequency

Suspensive hyphens
Use suspensive hyphens in a series when the individual items would have been hyphenated:
> We recommend a two-, three- or four-column format.

I.e.
Use *that is* instead.

In order to
Use *to* instead.

Input
Do not use as a verb. Use *enter* or *type* instead.

Insure
Use *insure* only for references to insurance. Use *ensure* to mean guarantee.

Italics
Use italics for emphasis, to introduce new terms, to set off letters and words, or to cite publications.

Italics for emphasis

Use italics for emphasis. Do not use boldface, underlining, quotation marks, or all caps to emphasize words:
> When emphasizing text, you should *not* use underlining.

Italics to introduce terms

Use italics the first time you introduce or define a new concept. The italics emphasize the word, and let readers know exactly what you are defining:
> A master file, called the *chapter file*, stores pointers...

You should also italicize foreign phrases not yet part of everyday English:
> Desktop publishing is now *de rigueur* in America's corporations.

Italics to set off letters, words, or phrases

Italicize references to letters, words, or phrases to set them off from the rest of the sentence, or to let the reader know you are treating the entire phrase as a group:
> Capitalize the *b*.
> The phrase *desktop publishing* is overused.

Italics to cite publications

Italicize the titles of books, magazines, newsletters, newspapers, plays, movies, and works of art.

Keys

Use the abbreviations shown below for the keys on a computer keyboard. Capitalize the first letter. Do not use italics, boldface, or all caps. Do not use an article preceding the name of a key:
> Instead of:
>> Press the Ctrl key.
>
> Use:
>> Press Ctrl.

Indicate simultaneous key combinations with a hyphen.
> Instead of:
>> Press Ctrl and D.
>
> Use:
>> Press Ctrl-D.

Key abbreviations

To maintain consistency, use the key abbreviations listed below:
> Alt
> Backspace
> Caps Lock
> Ctrl
> Ctrl-T (not ^T)
> Del
> End
> Enter
> Esc
> Home
> Ins
> Num Lock
> PgDn
> PgUp
> Shift
> Shift-Click
> Shift-Del
> Tab

Like versus such as

Use *like* to compare one thing to another:
> A good introduction is like a roadmap.

Use *such as* to connote *for example*:
> Application programs, such as word-processing and page-layout packages, are essential to desktop publishing.

Lists

You have many types of lists at your disposal. In general, you should keep bullet lists between three and seven items. For longer lists, use numbers so readers can keep track of the separate items.

Simple bullet lists

There are at least two kinds of simple bullet lists. A *sentence continuer* is a normal sentence that has been broken out into bullets for emphasis. Use a colon to end the main clause. The items should not be capitalized and they should not have any punctuation:

> The parts of a computer are:
> - a CPU
> - a monitor
> - one or more disk drives

The most common bullet list is a main clause followed by a colon. The items should not be capitalized and they should not have any punctuation at the end:

> You can do any of the following tasks quickly and easily:
> - writing
> - editing
> - printing
> - saving

Complex bullet lists

In complex bullet lists, the individual items are complete sentences (or very long phrases). Use upper and lower case and a period or semicolon at the end of each item:

> Here are a few things macros can accomplish:
> - They can save you the trouble of changing margins settings every time you want to type indented material.
> - They can provide you with automatic headings.
> - They can act as visible markers in the document.

Keep lists consistent. Make all the items complete sentences or all the items incomplete phrases, but do not mix the two.

Measurements
See *Numbers*.

Numbers

Numbers of nine or less
Spell out whole numbers from zero through nine.
> We suggest nine-point type...

Exception #1: Use numerals for numbers in a series, even if the numbers would be spelled out if used alone:
> Use 5, 10, or 15 picas.

Exception #2: Use numerals for everything in the sentence if you must use them for one item (in other words, be consistent within a sentence):
> We suggest 8-point type on 10-point line spacing.

Exception #3: Use numerals with units of measurement:
> $5 million
> 5%

Numbers of 10 or greater
Use numerals for whole numbers of 10 or greater:
> It is equal to 12 points...

Exception: Spell out numbers at the beginning of a sentence:
> Twenty-five key reasons...

Describing dimensions
Don't use spaces between figures describing the dimensions of an object. Use the lower case *x* with no spaces before or after to represent *by*:
> Use an 8.5x11 in. sheet of paper.

Fractions
For introductory and general material, use the general rule: Spell out numbers below 10, use numerals for numbers 10 and above:
> About three-fourths of all desktop publishers...

For technical material, use the actual fraction in numerical form:
   The left margin is ¾ of an inch wide.

Decimal fractions are acceptable for page sizes:
   A standard 8.5x11 in. page...

Inches
Use the abbreviation *in*.

Money
Use the same rules for money as for numbers in general. Spell out the numbers nine and under. Use numerals for 10 and above. If you spell out the number, spell out the unit of currency. If you use numerals, use a symbol for the currency. Do not use a decimal point for whole numbers:
   It's not worth two cents.
   The price has been raised to $895.
   The list price is $599.95.

Page sizes
You can refer to common sizes with decimal fractions. Use the lower case *x* to represent the word *by*:
   An 8.5x11 in. page...
   A 5.5x8.5 in. page...
   ...measures 51x66 picas...

Percentages
Use the numeral and the percent sign (%):
   The standard 5% rate...

Plurals of numbers
Form the plurals of spelled-out numbers like the plurals of nouns:
   Delete all the nines on the page.

Form the plurals of numerals by adding an *s* (no apostrophe needed):
   In the 1980s, desktop publishing has become the panacea for...
   They were in their 30s.

Numbers on the screen
When referring to numbers that appear on the screen, always use the numbering system just as it appears on the screen, even if it differs from the normal style. For instance, here are some Ventura examples:
>Add 06,00 picas...
>Increase the line spacing by 02.00 fractional pts...
>In From Left: 01,00 picas & points

Output
Do not use as a verb. Use *write*, *display*, or *print* instead.

Parentheses
Put punctuation *outside* the parentheses:
>A pica is equal to 12 points (about 1/6 inch) and is the standard unit...

Exception: A *detached* sentence. If the expression is a complete sentence that can stand on its own, put the punctuation inside the parentheses:
>... expressed in picas and points. (The measurements refer to the full-sized page.)

Parenthetical expressions
Parenthetical expressions interrupt the main clause:
>A pica is equal to 12 points (about 1/6 inch).

Setting parenthetical expressions apart
You have three ways to set the phrase apart: parentheses, commas, or em dashes. Your choice depends on the amount of emphasis you want:
>Use parentheses to whisper (when the phrase isn't crucial).
>Use commas, one on each side of the phrase, to talk in a normal voice.
>Use em dashes when — and only when — you want to talk loudly and emphasize the phrase.

Periods

Periods in captions
Do not use a period if the caption is a short label or title:
> Figure 2-2. Keyboard shortcuts

Use a period if the caption is a complete sentence:
> Use the keyboard shortcuts shown in the illustration above to speed editing in Ventura Publisher.

Periods and parentheses
Place the period outside the parenthesis:
> ... for the tags (for instance, Head1 and Head2).

Exception: Place the period inside if the parenthetical expression is a complete sentence that stands on its own:
> ... to generate an ASCII file. (Creating an ASCII file is usually as simple as printing a report to disk.)

Periods and quotation marks
Without exception, place the period inside quotation marks:
> Select the paragraph that begins "Justification overrides tab settings."

Question marks

Place question marks just as you place periods (inside quotation marks and outside parentheses):
> Desktop publishers often ask, "But what about downloadable fonts?"
> Are you ready to step up the pace (again)?

Exception #1: Place the question mark outside the quote marks if it is not part of the quotation:
> Have you ever heard them use the phrase "downloadable fonts"?

Exception #2: Place the question mark inside the parentheses if it is part of the parenthetical expression:
> He declares (and why should we doubt him?) that it is important to follow the rules of American usage.

Quotation marks

Quotation marks are rarely necessary. Use italics, not quotes, to signal new words or phrases. Use quotation marks only when you are actually quoting material, or if you are citing another chapter in your own book:
    Instead of:
        In this chapter you will meet the concept of the "chapter file."
    Try:
        In this chapter you will meet the concept of the *chapter file*.

Do not use quotation marks to set off cute or colloquial language. Do not use them after phrases such as *so-called* and *known as*. If the term is new or unfamiliar, use italics. If the term is merely a colloquialism, do not give it any special treatment. If you are afraid it will be misunderstood, substitute a more common phrase:
    Instead of:
        Let your word processor do the "heavy lifting."
    Try:
        Let your word processor do the heavy lifting.
    Or:
        Let your word processor do the hard work.

Punctuation and quotation marks

In general, periods, commas, and question marks go *inside* the quotation marks. Colons and semicolons go *outside* the quotation marks.

Semicolons

We recommend that you minimize the use of semicolons. However, they can be useful to separate phrases that have internal commas:
    Enter 1,582; 603; 170,040; and 17,381.

Single letters

Italicize single letters of the alphabet when used as a noun:
    Place the cursor in front of the *a* in the word apple.

Use an apostrophe to indicate the plural to avoid confusion:
> Instead of:
>> Capitalize all the *b*s.
>
> Try:
>> Capitalize all the *b*'s.

Such as

See *Like versus such as*.

That

The pronouns *which* and *that* are often confused and used incorrectly.

Which precedes an incidental thought. *Which* clauses are set off by a comma. Omitting the clause does not change the meaning of the sentence:
> The program has only two menus, which are short.
>> *(The program has only two menus. Their length is incidental.)*

That is a restrictive pronoun. *That* clauses are *not* set off by a comma, since the meaning of the sentence changes if you omit the clause:
> The program has only two menus that are short.
>> *(The program has many menus, but only two of them are short.)*

Test sentences by removing the clause. If the meaning does not change, use a comma and *which*. Otherwise, use *that*.

Verbs

Make sure the verb agrees with the true subject of the sentence:
> Incorrect:
>> The number of DTP packages have nearly doubled.
>
> Correct:
>> The number of DTP packages has nearly doubled.

Which

See *That*.

Sample Writing Guide 7

This chapter presents a sample writing guide — the one New Riders Publishing distributes to editors and authors. Much of the advice in this guide applies to all types of business writing. Still, some of it focuses more narrowly on the writing of computer books for the general public. Thus, although you may want to keep many of the same topics, you will probably need to change some of the specific suggestions.

As with the other samples in this book, use the following pages as a starting point. Add, delete, and modify as you see fit — the whole point is to come up with a succinct guide that is tailored to your own needs. If you purchased the optional Managing disk, you can start with the text files on the disk. If you use Xerox Ventura Publisher, you will also find chapter files and style sheets on the disk to duplicate our handbook.

For more about about the practicalities and politics of building an in-house handbook, see Chapter One, "Supervising Desktop Publishing." The remainder of this chapter duplicates the New Riders in-house writing guide.

New Riders' Writing Guide

This chapter is for those who want to improve their writing. We divided it into three sections:

- improving the organization —
  structuring your thoughts for easy comprehension

- improving the mechanics —
  developing the craft of writing

- improving the style —
  making your writing more vigorous

Over the past 50 years, a large body of work has appeared on how to improve writing. Much of it is based on scientific research into the habits of American readers. We haven't tried to duplicate that material here (in fact, we hope you will read the books and publications we recommend in the bibliography). We have simply addressed some of the toughest problems and possible solutions.

All of us who care about good writing struggled with these problems when we began our careers. The bad news: We're still struggling. Exercising your editing muscles is like exercising your body; the moment you stop, the flab starts to form again. But if you do a little each day, you can improve. You can master the self-discipline that turns bad writing into good. You can experience the pleasure of turning a fat, lazy sentence into a lean, mean idea machine.

Improving the organization

Organization has two essentials. The first is to start with a good outline. The second is to make your organizational scheme obvious to the reader. This section discusses both.

As long as the organization is solid, you can fix any other problems. But if the underlying structure is faulty, no amount of repair work can keep your book from collapsing into confusion. Organization has at least four important functions:

- It breaks a large topic into bite-size pieces.
- It shows how each part fits into the big picture.
- It helps readers find what they want.
- It lets readers customize the book by skipping sections they don't need.

Organize with an outline

Just as you wouldn't put up a house before finishing the foundation, you shouldn't start writing until you have perfected the outline. Review your outline with your editor until you are both satisfied. It will be the framework for your writing, a blueprint you refer to every day.

How do you put together a great outline? Simple: You concentrate on the *reader's* concerns. We recommend four steps:

1. Define the audience.
2. Determine your goal(s).
3. Choose an organizational method.
4. Build the outline.

The sooner you accomplish the first two tasks the better. They influence how you research and write. Remember: With today's computer books, the problem is rarely what to put in. More often it is what to leave out. The sooner you focus your efforts, the easier your job will be.

Defining the audience

How you define the audience determines the rest of your writing strategy. Be sure to spend enough time to come up with a clear, specific definition of your target market.

Users of the XYZ software package is *not* an adequate definition. What kinds of companies do these users work for? What jobs do they fill? What tasks do they perform with the software? You're not ready to start until you can answer these questions with confidence.

If you're not sure about the audience, do some research. Talk to your editor. Get in touch with the software designers and salespeople for their viewpoints. And call some users. Please. Some of our authors interview a dozen or more users before they start writing. There's no better way to get a handle on the real-world concerns of your eventual readers.

Take our word for it: You'll regret it if you skip this step. So will we, because your book won't be as good.

Determining your goal

Once you know who you're writing for, articulate what you want to do for them. This step may sound trite. In fact, it's extremely useful, as long as you are as specific as possible:

Bad:
  Help users of XYZ software.
Okay, but not great:
  Help beginning users learn XYZ.
Better:
  Help novice users learn to use XYZ to prepare three-dimensional graphs for presentations with a step-by-step, self-paced tutorial.

When you get to the outlining phase, you'll need to define your goal for each chapter as well.

If you write well enough, even the reader with no intrinsic interest in the subject will become involved.
                                                                    Tracy Kidder

Choosing an organizational method

Once you know your audience and what you want to do for them, you're ready to select the best method for organizing the material. Let's consider the main principles:

The organization of a computer book must make sense.

Not very controversial. Most writers and editors would agree. Yet as a writing aid, this statement is not very valuable.

The organization of a computer book must make sense to the reader.

This second version is more helpful. It makes the point that a book must be organized around the needs of the users, *not* around the program. But we can still expand the idea:

The organization of a computer book must make sense to the lowest common denominator of readers.

Now we're talking. Even if parts of your book delve into advanced topics, its *structure* should be apparent to a beginner. How can you make sure the organization will be helpful even to a novice? The easiest way is to organize the book to follow the reader's way of thinking.

Many writers stumble at this stage. They are so absorbed in the software that they organize according to the program's structure:

1. The File Menu
2. The Edit Menu
3. The Page Menu
4. The Frame Menu

This type of organization may have merit in a software manual. But New Riders' books go beyond — well beyond — product documentation. They must be organized according to readers' needs. And readers don't think in terms of menus and modules.

How *do* readers of computer books think? Those we've talked with think in terms of time, tasks, or skill levels. You should choose one (or more) of these three methods to organize your book.

One favorite way to organize is by time sequence. Chronological organization is easy for readers and writers alike. You start by discussing the first thing to do. Then you move on to the second step, and so on:

1. Starting the program
2. Creating your first document
3. Adding pictures to your document

Not every project lends itself to the chronological treatment. You can also organize around specific tasks:

1. Creating an invoice
2. Creating a newsletter
3. Creating a directory

This style guide is primarily organized by task. We start out with supervising desktop publishing, then move on to creating text, creating pictures, editing, and finally formatting. This method has certain advantages. People usually think in terms of their tasks. In addition, task-oriented organization lets readers pick and choose. They can study the job they need to do right now and leave the others for later. One disadvantage, however, is the tendency for the material to overlap, leading to repetition or excessive cross-referencing.

Finally, you can organize around skill levels. In this scheme, you present only what readers need to know at each phase.

1. Creating simple reports
2. Creating multi-column reports
3. Creating advanced reports with pictures

When organizing by skill level, you withhold some of the material until readers are ready for it. This method has the advantage of allowing users to get up and running right from the start, before they understand the advanced features. The more complex the program, the more likely it is that you will need to present material in stages.

Which of the three should you use? In practice, most books combine two or more. In the New Riders' book *Publishing Power with Ventura*, for example, we organized each chapter around a task (a report, a proposal, a newsletter, etc.). Then we grouped those tasks by skill level — the easiest documents first, the advanced later. Within each chapter, we organized by time sequence.

Building the outline

Outlining is one of the hardest parts of writing a book. It's where you have to grapple with the big issues: which chapters cover what topics, and in what order. Outlining begins, however, with a surprisingly simple principle:

Put all the material on one subject in the same place.

This general principle doesn't mean there can't be any overlap. You may need to remind readers of another section, paraphrase previous material, summarize key points, or insert cross-references. With these exceptions, however, one-stop-shopping should be the rule. Readers should be able to find everything they need in one place without jumping from chapter to chapter.

With that general principle in mind, you're ready to start writing the outline. Start with any method that helps you sort and categorize information: top-down charts, formal outlines, tree charts, cluster diagramming, or Warnier-Orr diagrams (Figure 7-1). Eventually, however, your editor will need something that resembles a table of contents (TOC): a list of chapters with their main headings.

Once you have grappled with the big issues, as we discussed earlier, your editor will probably recommend that you expand your first outline into a more detailed three- or four-level outline. He or she may also suggest that you write introductory paragraphs for each chapter and its major sections. In the beginning, however, a simple TOC will suffice.

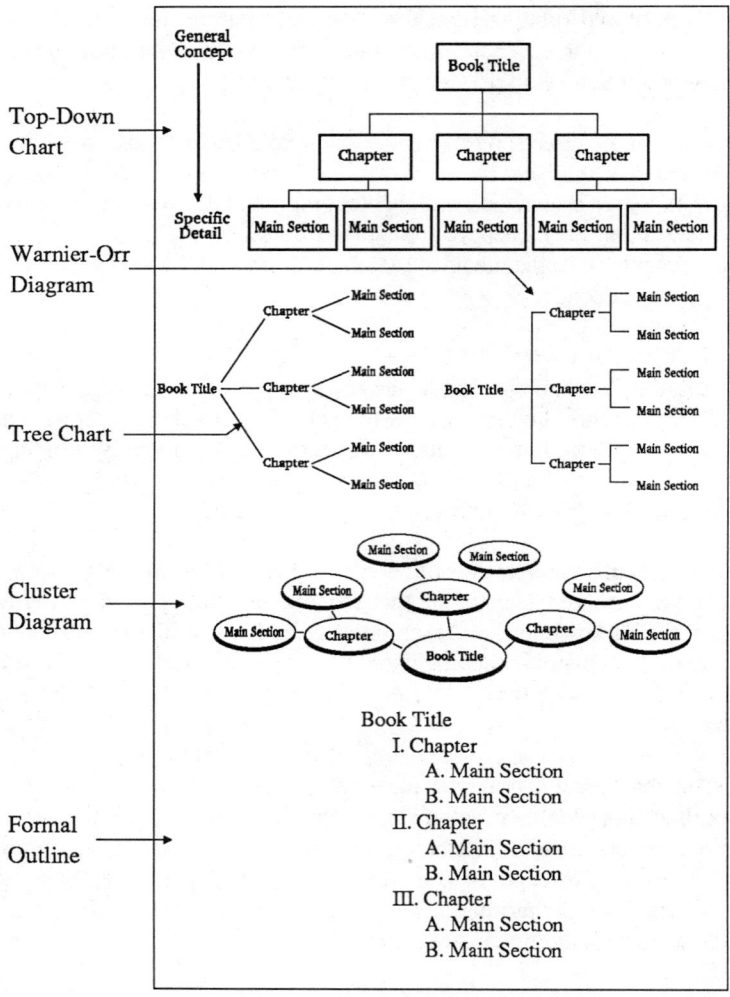

7–1. A few of the organizational techniques available to help you structure your book.

Keeping the structure easy to understand

As you build your outline, remember that your first objective is to help readers grasp the big picture. If you have more than eight or nine chapters, you should probably subdivide the book. Consider this book by way of example:

Without subdivisions:
1. Supervising Desktop Publishing
2. Creating Text
3. Creating Pictures
4. Editing
5. Formatting Pages
6. Sample Grammar and Usage Guide
7. Sample Writing Guide
8. Sample Tag Dictionary
9. Sample Checklists
10. Bibliography and Resources

With subdivisions
Part One — How-To
1. Supervising Desktop Publishing
2. Creating Text
3. Creating Pictures
4. Editing
5. Formatting Pages

Part Two — Reference
6. Sample Grammar and Usage Guide
7. Sample Writing Guide
8. Sample Tag Dictionary
9. Sample Checklists
10. Bibliography and Resources

It's easier to swallow after subdividing, don't you agree? Breaking long outlines into logical groupings helps to predigest the contents for readers.

Applying the structure

In the previous section, we emphasized the importance of building a good outline before you start writing. But your outline won't help readers much unless you make it obvious to them. You can do that with introductions, headings, and summaries.

Using introductions to explain the structure

If this were a book on journalism, we would talk about using the introduction to hook readers — to amaze, amuse, or otherwise entice them into reading an article. But since we are talking about computer books, the intro has a different job.

Pay attention — we are about to reveal a secret. Here is the advanced formula for technical writing used by the nation's top professionals:

1. Tell them what you are going to tell them.
2. Tell them.
3. Tell them what you told them.

This old saw from creative-writing class is as valid as ever. Not observing it is a common failing of modern technical writing.

The first step occurs in the introduction. If it does nothing else, an introduction should tell readers what's ahead. (If it also amuses or amazes them, so much the better.)

Most people don't read computer books from start to finish. They browse, they jump around, they skip straight to the section that deals with their current problem. Your book must accommodate these habits. You need an overall introduction to the book, of course, but you also need a brief intro for each chapter. Readers can skim the intros until they find the section they need. If your book has long chapters, you should also put a brief intro at the beginning of each subsection.

Read over your compositions and, when you meet a passage which you think is particularly fine, strike it out.
                                                            Samuel Johnson

The general introduction to a how-to computer book should usually follow this format:

1. Benefits of the program
   Give them a reason to read about it.

2. Benefits of the book
   Give them a reason to read about it in this book.

3. Audience and assumptions
   Tell them who the book was written for (beginners, advanced). Also tell them which software version the book covers, what equipment they will need, what they must know before they can use this book, and so on.

4. How to use the book
   Explain the major divisions. Indicate who should read which parts of the book.

The *How to use the book* section deserves extra discussion. Don't just march through a list of chapters. Think of it from (you guessed it) the *reader's* point of view. Tell beginners what they should do. Point out what advanced users should do differently. Explain how instructors can get the most out of it. You might even try putting all this in a table:

To Do This	Turn To These Chapters
Learn the Basics	Chapters One, Two, and Three
Master Advanced Topics	Chapters Four, Five, and Six
Customize the Program	Chapters Seven and Eight

Writing chapter introductions

Start every chapter with a brief overview: why they should read this chapter, what they will learn, how it is organized, which sections can be skipped by advanced users. (You can often accomplish some of these tasks with a list or a chapter table of contents.)

Introductions should be easy to create, but for some reason they often cause problems. Let's try to get to the heart of the matter: Your introduction should state your subject. Then it should list the key ideas of the chapter, in the sequence they will appear.

That's it. That's all it needs to do. Don't use the introduction for exceptions, qualifications, or details. Treat it as a brief summary and a roadmap. It doesn't have to be fancy, elaborate, or exceptionally creative as long as it gets the job done:

> This chapter explains how to add, edit, and delete text.

Different kinds of books need different chapter intros. Take reference books, for example. Each chapter must be self-contained. There is no guarantee the reader has studied the previous chapters. The introductions, therefore, must be self-contained as well. They must warn readers what knowledge they will need before they can tackle the material:

> This chapter explains how to add, edit, and delete text. Before you begin, you should know how to load the software and start a new document, as explained in the previous chapter.

Teaching guides are a different matter. In this case, you do readers a favor if you look backwards as well as forwards. In other words, remind them where they've been as well as where they are going. Help them keep the big picture in mind by showing how each chapter advances from the previous one and leads to the next:

> By now you know how to add and delete text. Next you will learn how to change its attributes — how to make it bold, italic, centered, and so on. This is the last chapter in Part One. Once you complete this section, you will have the skills to tackle the advanced exercises in Part Two.

Don't forget to mention benefits. Tell readers what they will gain. It takes a lot of effort to slog through a tutorial. Be sure to dangle the carrot before you apply the stick.

Long chapters need overviews for each major subsection. You may feel like you are repeating yourself. Fine. Some readers will go straight from the table of contents to the fourth subsection of the third chapter. Once they get there, they want to know, "Is this the right section? What does it cover?" So tell them.

Using titles and headings to signal the structure

You saw above how introductions can reveal the organization. If the introductions are the roadmaps, then the titles and headings are the signposts. They make it easy for readers to find their way around.

Earlier we recommended defining your goals. Here's another place to use that information. In technical writing, the most helpful titles are often nothing more than a restatement of the goal:
Using 1-2-3
Mastering WordPerfect
Getting It Printed

The same holds true for headings. As you thumb through this book, you'll see how we used this principle ourselves. Most of our headings simply summarize what you can expect to learn in that section.

Headings should be short and sweet. The short part isn't hard. Many writers, however, don't know how to sweeten things so headings are easier to swallow. Here are a few tips:

Use different levels of headings. Technical material benefits from headings that display the hierarchy of information. Each chapter has several main topics (first-level headings). Each main topic has several subtopics (second-level headings). In complex books, you may need third- or even fourth-level headings as well (Figure 7-2).

Each level should be clearly defined and distinct, so readers know at a glance where they stand. First-level headings should be bigger and bolder than second-level headings; which should be bigger than third-level headings; which should be bigger than the body text.

Use parallel construction for each level. You can also help to make the organization clear to the reader by using parallel construction. Parallel construction sends subtle signals that help orient the reader.

To understand why, consider how people become accustomed to signals. For instance, what do drivers do when they see a red octagon on a signpost? They stop. (OK, most of them stop. People from California slow

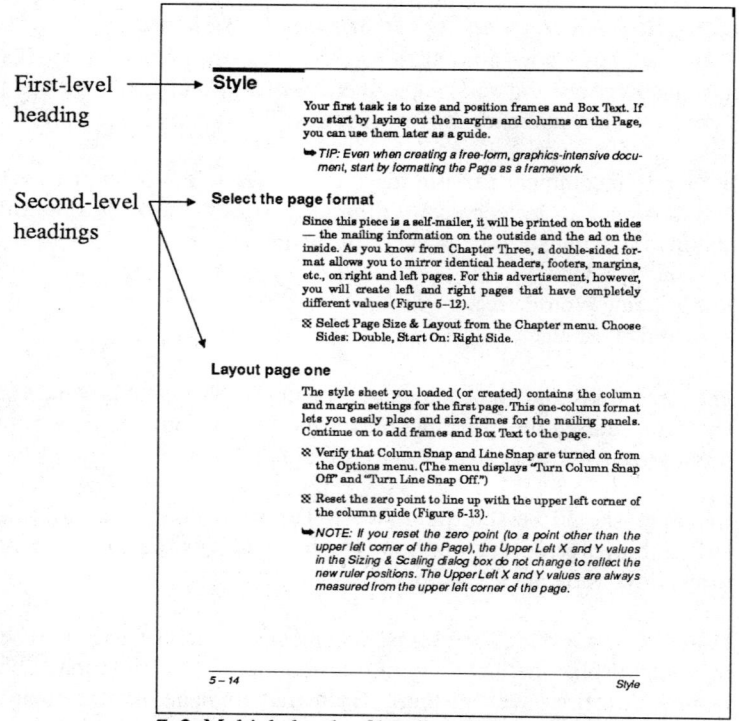

7-2. Multiple levels of headings help readers navigate through technical material.

First-level heading → **Style**

Second-level headings → **Select the page format**, **Layout page one**

down. A little.) But what if stop signs were inconsistent? What if some were green ovals? And others were blue squares? Obviously, they'd have much less worth as signals. In the same fashion, *headings are more valuable if they are consistent.*

Look over the six headings below. Try to figure out which ones are main headings and which ones are secondary:

File-management techniques
File creation
Naming conventions
Managing manuscripts
Organization
Manuscript submission guidelines

Now try again, this time with parallel construction:
   Managing files
      How to create a file
      How to name a file
   Managing manuscripts
      How to organize a manuscript
      How to submit a manuscript

The second example makes it apparent which topics are major and which are minor, even in the absence of numbers, indents, or formatting. Each level uses a consistent style. You can use this same technique to give clues to readers as they browse, flip, skim, and read through your book.

Make headings specific. Make headings as specific as possible. Tell readers exactly what they will learn to do in that section:
   Instead of:
      Graphic functions
   Try:
      Drawing circles and rectangles

Involve the reader. Choose phrases that imply a benefit, especially in beginning- and intermediate-level books. The three most useful techniques are *verbs*, *questions*, and the *five W's*. You can mix and match these techniques, as long as you keep parallel construction in mind.

Verbs involve the reader. They suggest that he or she will be learning to do real work, not just studying abstract functions. Verbs are specific. They tell exactly what the reader will learn to do:
   Instead of:
      The Alignment dialog box
   Try:
      Aligning text

Questions are also useful for headings (as long as you don't overdo them), because they involve the reader:
   Why page design?

The five W's (who, what, where, why, when, and how) are also a proven way to involve the reader while explaining exactly what's about to happen:
When to use frames
How to create a hanging indent

Using summaries to remind about structure

So far we've explained how to make the structure more obvious with introductions and headings. You can also reinforce the organization with summaries.

Not everyone bothers to read summaries. Nevertheless, you should consider including them for those who do. Some readers don't fully grasp the big picture until they've been through the chapter. The summary helps those people distill the details and fit them into the overall structure.

Most New Riders' books need chapter summaries. The more technical the material, the more likely a summary is required. At the very least, this summary should tell them what you told them. It can be a brief paragraph that sums up what you've covered and hints at what's coming up next. It can be a bulleted list of key points. It can be a detailed listing of the major tips and tricks covered in the chapter. Or it can be a combination of all these elements.

Testing the structure

Test the organization at the outline stage and again after you finish each chapter. It will help you spot how well you have organized and how apparent the structure is to the reader.

To see if you are doing a good job, list only the first-level headings of each chapter, as if you were creating a table of contents:
Chapter One
  Adding text
  Deleting text
  Copying and moving text
  Searching and replacing text

Readers should be able to make sense of every chapter just from its first-level headings, *even if they are not familiar with the subject of the book*. Try the test again after you've finished the first draft. If your word processor includes outlining, collapse the outline to the main headings. See if they make sense. Check for parallel construction. Now expand to the second-level headings and check them as well.

Improving the mechanics

The previous section dealt with overall organization. Now we'll move on to some of the details— the individual components that make up good technical writing:

- words
- sentences
- paragraphs
- transitions

A quick time-out. We're going to ask you to bear with us for a paragraph or two. We want to give you a brief motivational talk about writing.

For many people, good writing is a mysterious, unfathomable occurrence. In our opinion, *great* writing is indeed mysterious. But *good* writing — clear, crisp, everyday prose — is something you can learn.

Good technical writing involves a few basic techniques. Most of them are mentioned in this chapter. With a bit of practice, almost anyone can learn to apply these techniques to their writing and editing.

Now for the lecture we warned you about. Getting better takes practice. For some reason, the idea of practicing seems foreign to many writers. They seem to forget that great tennis players (to name just one example) practice four or five hours per day. There are only six basic shots in tennis. That means that top players practice those same six fundamentals dozens of times each day. Hundreds of times each week. Thousands of times each month.

You can become very good the same way tennis pros do — by drilling the fundamentals over and over again. Some writers begin a new book by reviewing one or two of the classic reference guides. Others start each day by reading a page or two of style advice. Still others focus on one specific skill during each project — cutting the fat, say, or improving transitions. Then they choose a new area to concentrate on for the next project.

Whatever works for you. The point is, there's no mystery to becoming a good writer. Plain old hard work does the trick.

End of lecture. The rest of this section revolves around the mechanics of writing — those fundamental techniques that professionals practice over and over again.

Words

Words are your tools. As you build your book, be sure to use the right ones for the job. Here are five tips:

1. Prefer short words to long

Don't use a long word when a short one will do. Computer books are tough enough without adding the burden of long Latin words. The suffixes *tion*, *ite*, *ize*, *ility*, and *ment* are clues that you have fallen into the trap:
Instead of:
> Finalization of these six preliminary requirements is a prerequisite of commencement of system utilization.

Try:
> You have to do all six before you can start using the system.

Instead of:
> Utilize the To Print dialog box to implement the report printing function.

Try:
> Use the To Print dialog box to print the report.

So please: Eschew pretentious Latinate diction.

2. Prefer the specific to the abstract
Generalities make for dull reading. Favor specific nouns instead:
> Instead of:
>> The output device may take a long time to produce the first page.
>
> Try:
>> The printer may take up to five minutes to produce the first page.

Authors use words to paint pictures in the reader's mind. The more abstract the words, the fainter the picture. Specific words conjure up an immediate impression. Abstract words have to be translated by the reader.

3. Avoid vague antecedents
Stay away from vague pronouns that don't refer to anything in particular, especially as the subject of the sentence. To improve your writing, eliminate these phrases, substitute a word, or rewrite the sentence:
> Instead of:
>> It has been determined that the easiest way to...
>
> Try:
>> The easiest way to...
>
> Instead of:
>> This means you should never start the program before...
>
> Try:
>> Never start the program before...
>
> Instead of:
>> It will be clear that printing a document requires...
>
> Try:
>> Clearly, printing a document requires...
>
> Instead of:
>> There are several reasons why the Alignment dialog box is important.
>
> Try:
>> The Alignment dialog box is important for several reasons. First...

Watch for the tendency to finish a long paragraph with a vague pronoun:
> This allows you to index the document without...

A work of art is work.

If you have described several things in the paragraph, the reader has no way of knowing what *This* refers to. The last item? All of the items together? Avoid confusion. Restate the subject to make the sentence clear:
>This command allows you to index the document without...
>The actions described above allow you to index the document without...
>The Multi-Chapter dialog box allows you to index the document without...

4. Minimize adverbs and adjectives
Avoid adjectives and adverbs, especially weak qualifiers like *very, completely, somewhat,* and so on. Use better verbs and nouns instead, or try to be more specific:
>Instead of:
>>The printer took a very, very long time to produce the page.
>
>Try:
>>The printer took ten minutes to produce the page.
>
>Or even:
>>The printer choked on the page.

Adjectives and adverbs are the spinach of technical prose (to paraphrase Robert Benchley). Everybody says they're good for you, but nobody would miss them if they disappeared. Let your verbs and nouns do the heavy lifting. Relegate adverbs and adjectives to their proper role as occasional assistants. As Strunk and White put it, qualifiers like *rather, very,* and *little* are "the leeches that infest the pond of prose, sucking the blood of words."

Avoid cliches
Avoid cliches ~~like the plague~~.

Sentences
Once you've got the words right, you're ready to string them into sentences. The following six techniques will help.

1. Prefer active voice to passive
The passive voice robs writing of strength. It's the stuff of bureaucratic memos and self-inflated lawyers. Moreover, passive voice can be the symptom of some dangerous problems.

If you are thinking more about the product than the reader, you tend to say: "The program can be started by...." When you take the user's point of view, you switch naturally to active voice: "You can start the program by..." or "Start the program by...."

Writers also tend to adopt the passive when they talk down to readers:
> Drawings should be created at twice the size of the frame they will occupy. Annotation text should be drawn at twice the size intended for the finished illustration.

Passive prose distances the writer from the reader. It turns the author into an authority figure, rather than a friend who's passing on some good tips. A better strategy is to treat readers like you would treat your friends:
> You can tell them directly what to do:
>> Create drawings at twice the size of the frame they will occupy.
>
> Or you can make recommendations:
>> We suggest that you draw annotation text twice the intended size...

The passive voice does have its place. You can't (and shouldn't) eliminate every passive sentence. But the more active sentences you use, the more vigorous your writing.

You can spot passive voice by looking for sentences where something is done to the subject. Usually they include some form of the verb *to be*:
> The file names will be displayed...
> Potential problems may be encountered during the initial phase.

By contrast, the subject does something in an active sentence:
> The screen lists the file names...
> You may have problems at the start.

To make your sentences active, get in the habit of saying who does what:
> Users often have trouble with...
> You can create this effect by...
> Ventura accepts text files from...
> We recommend that you...

If you are writing a tutorial, don't be afraid to use the imperative in place of the passive:
> Instead of:
>> The header should be turned off for the first page of the chapter.
>
> Try:
>> Turn off the header for the first page of the chapter.

2. *Use present tense*

Try to stay in the present tense. You don't want a scholarly dissertation on theoretical possibilities: what *will* happen, *could* happen, *might* happen, *should* happen. Instead, you want to give the impression that you are right there with the reader:
> Instead of:
>> As soon as you have entered the command, the screen will display the Item Selector.
>
> Try:
>> As soon as you enter the command, the screen displays the Item Selector.
>
> Or:
>> Enter the command. The screen displays the Item Selector.

The present tense complements the active voice and friendly tone we seek in our books. Naturally, you will find many cases where it is necessary to switch tenses. But try to stay in the present tense as much as possible, especially when giving instructions.

3. *Keep sentences short*

Short sentences make complex material easier to understand. Often, the easiest way to improve a beginning writers' prose is to divide their long sentences into shorter ones. To do this, you may have to restate the subject, or rephrase it as a pronoun:
> One sentence:
>> As Ventura builds a document, it uses different files to hold information, some of which are named by the user (text files, for example) and some by Ventura (caption files, for instance).
>
> Three sentences:
>> As Ventura builds a document, it uses different files to hold informa-

tion. Some of these document files are named by the user (text files, for example). Others are named by Ventura (caption files, for instance).

Don't fall into the trap of making every single sentence a short one. But take a careful look at anything over 20 words and see if splitting it will improve the clarity.

4. Keep the subject close to the verb

Every sentence answers two key questions: 1) *what am I talking about?* (subject) and 2) *what am I saying about it?* (verb). When you separate the subject and verb too much, you make it hard to find the meaning:

> This section, which explains how Ventura builds documents and the differences between Ventura's style sheets and its chapter files, is the key to unlocking the full power of the program.

Try to rearrange or split the sentence to make it's meaning more apparent:

> This section is the key to unlocking the full power of the program. It explains how Ventura builds documents. It also clarifies the differences between Ventura's style sheets and its chapter files.

5. Avoid wordiness

Cut unnecessary words from your sentences:

> Instead of:
>> Many of today's users have a tendency to agree that there are only two programs in the area of desktop publishing that truly stand out.
>
> Try:
>> Many users agree that only two desktop-publishing programs stand out.

6. Vary sentence length

Some writers rarely vary sentence length. Each sentence follows the same pattern. Yes, you should prefer short, simple sentences over complicated ones. But that doesn't mean you can't have long sentences when needed. Or short ones.

Paragraphs

The paragraph is the basic unit of thought. It should be handled differently in technical books than in articles and fiction. Here are three tips for better paragraphs:

1. Use short paragraphs

Technical material is difficult, so divide it into short, digestible pieces. Don't face readers with an unbroken sea of gray type. In general, keep paragraphs between two and ten sentences in length. And don't be afraid to use an occasional one-sentence paragraph for emphasis.

Try it.

2. Use topic sentences

Like all good things, a paragraph should have a beginning, a middle, and an end. The first or second sentence of the paragraph should summarize the paragraph. Typically, the rest of the sentences are examples or explanations that amplify the topic sentence. For example, take another look at the previous paragraph in this section:

> Technical material is difficult, so divide it into short, digestible pieces (*topic sentence*). Don't face readers with (*explanation*)...In general, keep paragraphs (*example*)...And don't be afraid to (*example*)...

3. Use transitions

Not every paragraph needs a transition. Still, if you look for opportunities to use them, you will find that they give your writing better flow and cohesiveness.

The idea is simple enough. You want each paragraph to relate to the ones before and after. If a paragraph is part of a sequence, you want the reader to know it:

> Next you will learn how to create headers and footers.
> Another benefit from the CAD model is...

Likewise, if the paragraph illustrates a point made earlier, you want to make that obvious:

> For instance, electronic drafting allows you to...
> As we saw above, the Sizing & Scaling dialog box...

Transitions show relationships. They may show how a paragraph relates to other paragraphs nearby. They may introduce a new topic. Or they may refer to the overall structure. Transitions usually occur at the beginning of a paragraph, but they sometimes work just as well at the end:
> The following section demonstrates how to use this function to create page numbers.

Often, a transition is nothing more than a word or two at the beginning of a paragraph:
> Clearly, it helps to focus on...

In other cases, a transition may be a phrase, a sentence, or a paragraph. The beginning of a new section or topic often requires a longer transition.
> So far we have seen how to choose hardware for a CAD system. Now let's turn our attention to...

If transitions are one of your weak points, try making a separate pass through the manuscript during which you do nothing but add transitions. Table 5-1 lists dozens of possibilities by category.

Table 5-1. Transitions by category

Cause	That is
Clearly	This being so
Evidently	In these circumstances
Here's why	One example is
It follows that	These are some of
Just as predicted	One of the toughest parts of
Just as you might expect	In particular
No wonder	First
Which leads us to	Then
For this reason	These observations imply
	Consider this puzzling question
Examples	The best way to describe
In fact	Four elements of a
For example	Yes
For instance	No
To illustrate	To that end

Table 5-1, continued.

Intensifying
  Certainly
  Clearly
  Even
  Evidently
  Indeed
  In fact
  Of course
  Remember
  Undoubtedly

Introductions
  To that end
  "What's in it for me?" you ask?
    Good question. Mr. XXX has an answer.
  A closer inspection might reveal
  How, you might ask, did
  Just as predicted

Opposing
  But
  By contrast
  Conversely
  Even though
  For all that
  However
  Nevertheless
  On the other hand
  Otherwise
  Remember
  Still
  Though

Series/sequence
  Accordingly
  After
  Already
  Also
  And there's more
  And
  Before
  Besides
  Finally
  First
  Formerly
  Furthermore
  Here again
  In addition
  Later
  Likewise
  Looking ahead
  Meanwhile
  Moreover
  Most important
  Moving right along
  Next
  Once again
  On top of that
  Second
  Similarly
  Subsequently
  Then
  Until recently
  We now come to
  What's more
  Which leads us to
  With that out of the way
  Yet another

Table 5-1, continued.

Summing Up
  Accordingly
  Apparently
  As a result
  Certainly
  Clearly
  Consequently
  Evidently
  Finally
  For
  For this reason
  For all that
  In brief
  In conclusion
  In short

It follows that
Let's look at the record
Presumably
Notwithstanding
Simply stated
So don't forget
So remember
So
Therefore
There you have it
The result?
This being so
To sum up
Undoubtedly
What does this mean for you?

Consistency

The easiest way to confuse people is to be inconsistent.

Consistency reassures readers. It also makes your book easier to use. New Riders' books are business tools. Readers want to concentrate on the subject, not on the amazing variety of your spelling, punctuation, synonyms, and style. Here are some of the key areas your book must remain consistent with:

1. **The product.** This is the first and foremost rule. Your book must match what readers see on their screens and in their product manuals. If the product spells things wrong, then your book has to spell them wrong.

2. **Standard American English.** Chapter 6, "Sample Grammar and Usage Guide," provides basic rules you should follow.

3. **Its own organization.** If the first chapter is organized with definition first, then procedure, then example, every chapter should follow the same pattern.

4. **Its own terms.** If you use three different words to mean the same thing, readers will try to puzzle out the significance of the variations. Pick one word and stick with it. It may seem repetitive, but it helps the users. Don't call it the *screen* one place, and the *monitor* or the *video display* somewhere else. Don't capitalize *ENTER* in one place and use *Enter* in another.

What do you do when there are several different words for the same concept? For the answer to that question, return to item number one in the list above.

Improving the style

Welcome to the bonus round.

If you follow the advice in the previous two sections, you will already be ahead of the game. But if you're determined to go for the gold, you may also want to consider the additional subjects discussed below. Professional writers spend a lifetime mastering the subtleties of good prose. In this short space, we can't do more than point you in the right direction. With that caveat, we offer three ways to make your writing come alive:

- Improving the tone
- Using examples and comparisons
- Adding humor

William Sloane said, "There are no uninteresting subjects, only uninteresting writers." Of course, Old Man Sloane never had to explain the schematics of an Intel coprocessor chip. Still, there are several steps you can take to make technical writing more readable.

> *Brevity is only skin deep, and the world is full of thin-skinned people.*
>
> Richard Armour

Improving the tone

The tone is the manner in which you express yourself:

- friendly
- formal
- emotional
- impartial

Why worry about the tone of your writing? For the answer, ask yourself how you would prefer to learn. From a robot that churns out one mechanical sentence after another? From a know-it-all expert who talks down to you? Or from a friend who has suffered through the same frustrations and is passing on a few tips to ease the pain? Here are a few ways to improve the tone of a computer book:

Use a conversational style
At the heart of good writing — including good technical writing — there is a personal transaction. Ultimately, you must sell not only the subject matter, but yourself.

Imagine that you are sitting across from several friends. (For some of us, that means imagining that we actually *have* several friends.) How would you talk to them? That's how you should sound on paper too. Adopting this attitude will add warmth, accessibility, and brevity to your writing.

Don't be afraid to put yourself into the picture. Add personal observations and opinions. As long as you don't overdo it, feel free to admit that, yes, a human being did write this book:
   I realize that...
   We can't guarantee that you won't make any mistakes, but we...

Write freely and as rapidly as possible and throw the whole thing on paper. Never correct or rewrite until the whole thing is down. Rewrite in process is usually found to be an excuse for not going on.
                                                                John Steinbeck

A conversational style puts readers at ease. Even when you don't refer to yourself directly (and you shouldn't too often), you can still imply your presence. Describe things. Use your senses. Write as if you are sitting next to the reader:
> The disk drive will make a lot of noise during this operation. Don't be concerned.
>
> Surprised by the slow redrawing time? Some computers...

Use the second person

Talk directly to readers. Feel free to use words like "users" or "operators" when you are generalizing. But when you are telling them specifically what to do, use the second person (the word *you*). Read the next two passages and decide which one you'd prefer to read for 600 pages or so:
> After the user completes the backup procedure, the diskette should be stored in a safe location. If the user does not heed this advice, the diskette may become damaged and the information stored on it may be lost forever.
>
> After you finish backing up, store the disk in a safe place. Otherwise, you may lose the information.

Write from the reader's point of view

Most readers share three beliefs: that the IRS is out to get them (it is), that their boss is out to get them (he/she probably is), and that the computer is out to get them (it isn't, but who can blame them for wondering?). Want to know the secret of making friends with your readers? Simple: *Act like you're on their side.* Acknowledge problems. Confess to potential confusion. If you present the reader with a difficult challenge, admit it:
> At first the different cursor shapes may confuse you.
>
> Many people consider this the hardest part of learning the program (we certainly do).
>
> You may have trouble mastering this process the first time through. Don't give up. This command is the key to mastering...

I have rewritten — often several times — every word I have ever published. My pencils outlast their erasers.
Vladimir Nabokov

Don't qualify

Yes, you want to be friendly, but you also want to sound like you know what you are talking about. Avoid qualifying your statements too often. If you don't know what you are talking about, then avoid the subject altogether:

> Instead of:
>> The Item Selector would seem to be one of the best ways to navigate among subdirectories.
>
> Try:
>> The Item Selector is the best way to navigate among subdirectories.

If you're really not sure, do a little research until you are. Readers pay good money for your book(s) because they think you're an expert. Act like one.

Cut the fat

Be concise.

Using examples and comparisons

If there's one thing that marks boring technical writing, it is the lack of examples and comparisons. These two writing devices provide reference points and bring the writing closer to the readers' own experiences.

An *example* illustrates a point with a real-life case history. Examples bring instructional material to life. They help readers put theory to practice. You can integrate examples into the text or, as we have often done in this style guide, you can set them apart with special formatting:

> This is an example of an example. Notice the special formatting that signals the reader.

> *The first and most important thing of all, at least for writers, is to strip the language clean, to lay it bare down to the bone.*
> Ernest Hemingway

A *comparison* contrasts one thing with another. You can use similes, metaphors or analogies. A *simile* compares with the words *like* or *as*:
> An introduction is like a roadmap.

A *metaphor* contains an implied comparison:
> Ventura is the heavyweight champion of the desktop-publishing arena.
> Headings are signposts that mark the way for readers.

An *analogy* is like an extended metaphor. It compares things from two different categories. In this style guide, for instance, we imply that a book is like a journey. We then compare introductions to roadmaps, headings to signposts, and so on.

You don't have to know the definitions of similes, metaphors, and all the rest, but you do need plenty of examples and comparisons throughout your manuscript. If your first draft has sections that are unclear, try solving the problem with an example or a comparison.

Adding humor

Use humor if you can carry it off. Otherwise, don't. Please.

Humor isn't essential. You don't need punchlines to have a good computer book. However, if you feel you have a flair, go for it. Humor is especially helpful for defusing difficult and frustrating situations. When you know you are about to put readers through some pain, try making light of it:
> On the fun scale, indexing a book ranks somewhere between an audit and a root canal. Nevertheless...

Knowing when and how to use humor is probably more instinct than anything else. On the other hand, knowing when *not* to use humor is something you can learn. Don't let humor get in the way of your book's main purpose. The goal of a computer book is to make life easier for readers. Abandon any jokes that could make their lives *more* difficult.

For instance, don't use clever titles and headings unless you are *positive* they convey the content. Don't damage their value as signposts for the sake of a witticism. Your headings may be the only thing the reader goes on when looking for information.

Suppose you are a busy professional. You need to download fonts to a laser printer. You've got a deadline and the boss is breathing down your neck. You reach for a reference book and turn to the chapter on fonts and printing. Would you know where to look based on the following headings:
Don't Be Type-Cast!
Tale of the Type
About Face!
How to Put Your Best Font Forward
That's Font-astic!

In general, then, stay away from humor in headings. You should also avoid forced humor anywhere in the manuscript. You can easily overdo the "Aren't we having fun!?!" thing. Yes, you should periodically encourage and congratulate the reader. But please avoid ersatz enthusiasm:
Isn't dimensioning polygons fun!?!
Good job! You turned on your computer by yourself! Are you ready to learn even more about your exciting new machine! Let's get started, shall we!

Continuing on

We've reached the end of our chapter on writing style. We've examined a few ways to improve the structure, the mechanics, and the style of your prose. Let's go over the main points again:

- Build your book on the solid foundation of a strong outline, one that reflects the reader's point of view.

- Words are your tools. Choose them with care. Make them as short and specific as possible.

- Stack your words into sentences, and your sentences into logical paragraphs. Then bind the paragraphs together with transitions.
- To give your work the finishing touch, strive constantly to perfect your writing style.

If you're dedicated to the proposition of improving yourself, you are just beginning. You will take these brief hints and use them as a starting point for further study.

Tips for improvement

One way to improve is to read good writing. The front page feature stories of the *Wall Street Journal*, for instance, are almost always well-written. Try reading them twice — once for content, a second time to examine the writing. Try to break the story down into its components. Watch for leads, hooks, transitions, and other devices you can borrow.

It's equally important to read examples of good *technical* writing. Apple manuals are often (but not always) well-written. You might also pick up a few of the all-time computer bestsellers. Not all of them are sterling examples throughout, but all of the top sellers contain material you can learn from. To get the most out of your reading, examine how the best authors solve problems similar to your own. If you are faced with a chapter introduction, for instance, take a look at four or five books. See how they did it. Notice the order in which they introduce material. Imitate the approaches you like. Likewise, study how other authors handle these common trouble spots:
- step-by-step instructions
- section intros and roadmaps
- transitions
- examples
- integrating illustrations and tables

When I was starting out, I often outlined entire articles and chapters by other authors. I would jot a code letter in the margin to indicate what the writer was doing: *I* for intro, *E* for example, *T* for transition, and so on. In this fashion, I was able to unearth the underlying framework that held everything together.

Here's another tip that will help you improve: Try editing other people's work. As you edit, you will be forced to articulate problems and suggest solutions. In your attempt to help someone else, you will find yourself grappling with gray areas, looking up definitions, and searching for remedies — those oh-so-important activities that you never have time to do when locked in battle with a blank piece of paper (or, more accurately, a blank screen). In my opinion, there's no better way to learn than by teaching someone else.

If you get good enough at editing others, you will eventually be able to do something even more difficult: edit yourself.

Need a place to start? Try editing this handbook. How well did we take our own advice? You might begin by answering these questions:

- Did the organization work? Is the material broken up in the way that is most useful to readers?
- Were chapter and section introductions handled well? Did they give you the clues you needed?
- Where were you confused? Which sections should be rewritten or expanded?
- What other aids (charts, tables, illustrations) would help authors do their job more quickly and efficiently?
- Did you notice any irritating stylistic quirks or habits that got in the way?

Make your notes in the margins, then photocopy those pages and send them back in. You'll never have a better chance to get even with an editor.

Jesse Berst
March 1989

Sample Tag Dictionary

8

This chapter overviews the tag system we use at New Riders. In the next few pages, you'll find an abbreviated list of the tags we use most often, as well as samples of typical pages. If you need a more complete description, the tag dictionary later in the chapter provides a detailed explanation and a sample of each tag. In a few cases, we've included word processor and desktop publishing examples to illustrate complex effects.

The New Riders tag system

We designed our tag-naming conventions to make tagging as painless as possible. A uniform system makes it possible for a variety of authors, editors, formatters and designers to work on the same project.

The first segment of the tag name (approximately four letters) is the category. Thus, BodyBold and BodyCourier are both in the Body Text category, while ListRound and ListNumber are in the List category. We anchored the category at the beginning of the tag name for two reasons: to make it easy to remember where to look for the tag you need, and to group choices for related functions alphabetically.

The remainder of the name elaborates on the tag's purpose or attributes. For example, Body Text is normal body type while BodyBold is (you guessed it) bold and BodyCourier is a typewriter-style typeface.

As with any system, the key to the success of our tag-naming convention is consistency. While we've included enough tag names for most documents, you may discover you need to add a new tag. If this occurs, *stick to the system*. Your tag's function will be clear to everyone who needs to use it. If you have a question, *call your editor*.

The only exceptions are tags Ventura generates, such as Body Text and the Z_ tags (Z_Caption, Z_Box Text, etc.), where we don't have any control over the naming.

The Tag List

On the next page you'll find an abbreviated list of New Rider's most important tags and their functions. For a more detailed explanation or to see a sample, turn to the alphabetical tag dictionary that follows.

For convenience many of our authors set up macros, or keyboard shortcuts, for the tags they use most often. We have left space in the center column for you to fill in yours. (If you don't want to go to the trouble of writing macros, check with your editor. We may already have them set up for your word processor.)

New Riders tag list

Tag Name	Macro	Description
Body Text and variations		
Body Text		default condition, do not pretag
BodyCourier		text seen/entered by reader
BodySetIn		set in from left margin
BodyBold		bold face for emphasis
Captions		
Z_Caption		picture caption
Callouts		
Z_Box Text		callouts
Headings and Titles		
Head1		first level heading
Head2		second level heading
Head3		third level heading
HeadChap		chapter title, follows chapter number
HeadChapNum		chapter number
Lists		
ListRound		round bullet
ListBoxSolid		solid box bullet
ListBoxHollow		hollow box bullet
List2Col1		2-column list with bullet, first column
List2Col2		2-column list with bullet, second column
List2ColLast		2-column list with bullet, last column
ListNumber		auto-numbered list
Notes		
Note		important information
NoteWarn		warning of dangerous condition
Other		
PictureMark		picture location marker
DateMark		date of last edit
Tables		
TableHead		title of a table
Z_Tbl_Beg		beginning of a table
Z_Tbl_End		end of table

Change the rectangle's attributes ◄──────── Head2

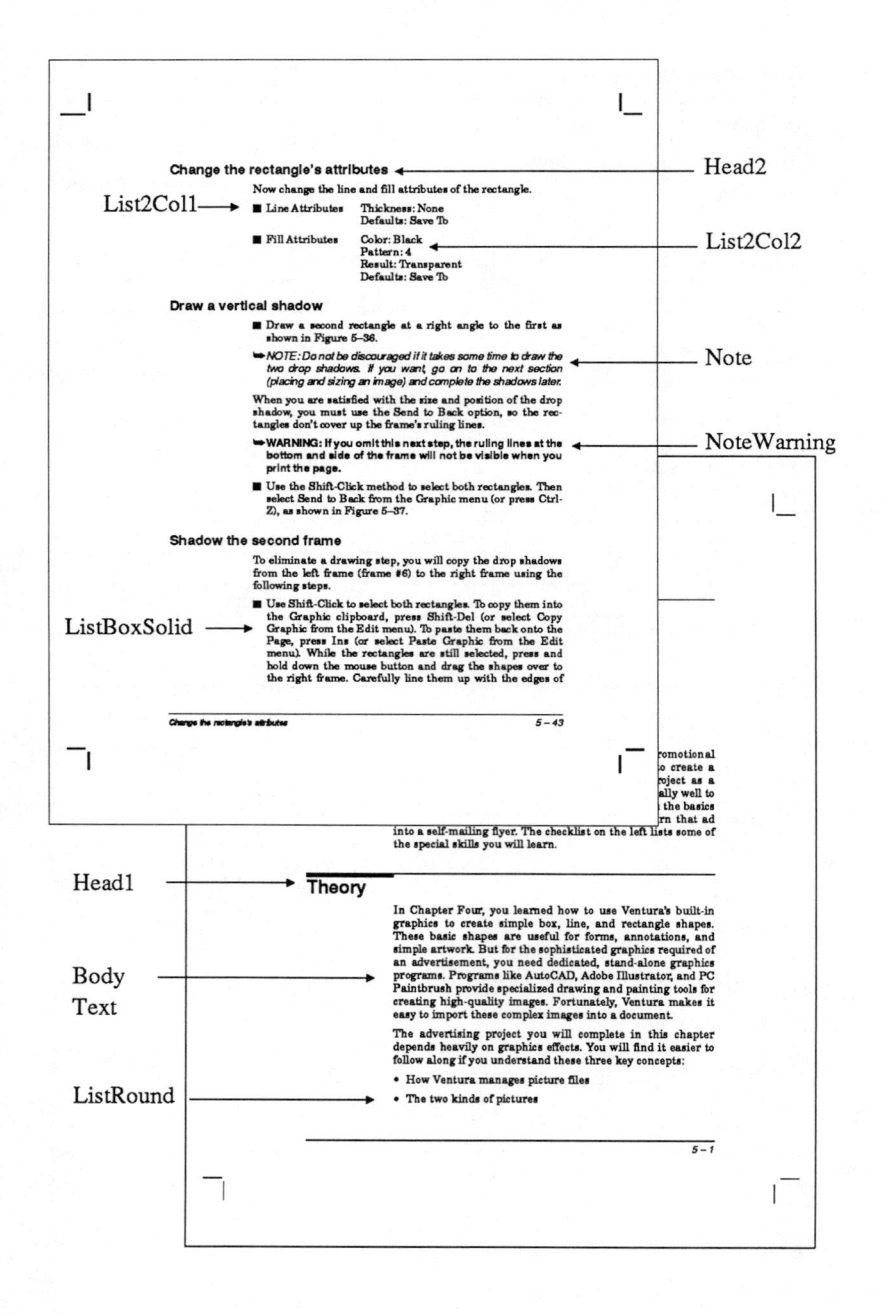

Now change the line and fill attributes of the rectangle.

List2Col1 ──►
- Line Attributes   Thickness: None
  Defaults: Save To
- Fill Attributes   Color: Black ◄──────── List2Col2
  Pattern: 4
  Result: Transparent
  Defaults: Save To

Draw a vertical shadow

- Draw a second rectangle at a right angle to the first as shown in Figure 5-36.

➥ *NOTE: Do not be discouraged if it takes some time to draw the two drop shadows. If you want, go on to the next section (placing and sizing an image) and complete the shadows later.* ◄──────── Note

When you are satisfied with the size and position of the drop shadow, you must use the Send to Back option, so the rectangles don't cover up the frame's ruling lines.

➥ **WARNING: If you omit this next step, the ruling lines at the bottom and side of the frame will not be visible when you print the page.** ◄──────── NoteWarning

- Use the Shift-Click method to select both rectangles. Then select Send to Back from the Graphic menu (or press Ctrl-Z), as shown in Figure 5-37.

Shadow the second frame

To eliminate a drawing step, you will copy the drop shadows from the left frame (frame #6) to the right frame using the following steps.

ListBoxSolid ──►
- Use Shift-Click to select both rectangles. To copy them into the Graphic clipboard, press Shift-Del (or select Copy Graphic from the Edit menu). To paste them back onto the Page, press Ins (or select Paste Graphic from the Edit menu). While the rectangles are still selected, press and hold down the mouse button and drag the shapes over to the right frame. Carefully line them up with the edges of

---

...romotional ...o create a ...roject as a ...ally well to ...the basics ...rn that ad into a self-mailing flyer. The checklist on the left lists some of the special skills you will learn.

Head1 ──►
Theory

Body Text ──►
In Chapter Four, you learned how to use Ventura's built-in graphics to create simple box, line, and rectangle shapes. These basic shapes are useful for forms, annotations, and simple artwork. But for the sophisticated graphics required of an advertisement, you need dedicated, stand-alone graphics programs. Programs like AutoCAD, Adobe Illustrator, and PC Paintbrush provide specialized drawing and painting tools for creating high-quality images. Fortunately, Ventura makes it easy to import these complex images into a document.

The advertising project you will complete in this chapter depends heavily on graphics effects. You will find it easier to follow along if you understand these three key concepts:

ListRound ──►
- How Ventura manages picture files
- The two kinds of pictures

Body Text and variations

Body Text

Description and usage
Ordinary body copy. Use Body Text for the main text of the book.

Because Body Text is generated by Ventura, we have no control over its name. Thus, it is one of the few New Riders tags to contain a space. Ventura defaults to Body Text, so it is unnecessary to pretag it.

Formatted example

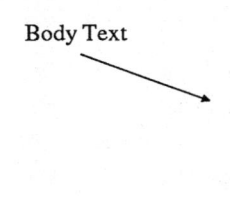

> Body Text
>
> Body text is the default condition in most desktop publishing programs. It is wise to assign attributes to body text before adding new tags, since it is the foundation for many other text elements.

BodyBold

Description and usage
Bold version of body text. Use to emphasize short paragraphs.

Reserve BodyBold for critical information. Do not use for multiple or long paragraphs. Before using, make sure Note or NoteWarn isn't more suitable for your application.

Formatted example

> BodyBold →
>
> Prior to the introduction of desktop publishing, graphic design was the domain of the skilled typesetter or designer. Now it is suddenly a concern of secretaries.
>
> **Therein lies the inherent danger of desktop publishing: It will not turn word processing specialists into designers.**
>
> To help ease this dilemma, New Riders Publishing has released a series of style sheets and accompanying books for novice desktop publishers. By providing style sheets for a variety of uses, these desktop publishing accessories put graphic design back in the hands of the designers, where it belongs.

BodyCourier

Description and usage

Typewriter text. Use for computer prompts and commands.

Use *only* to set off anything readers type on the keyboard or see on the screen. Any time readers see this typeface, they should expect to take action. Type in exactly what you want readers to type, since most will blindly mimic whatever they see. If you don't want them to type a period, don't put one at the end of the phrase.

Formatted example

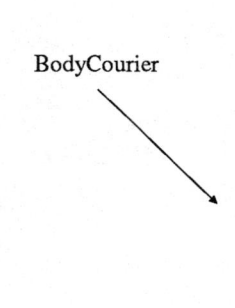

BodyCourier

To save formatting time, text may be pretagged in any compatible word processor. For example, to tag a paragraph as a third level heading (Head3), enter:

```
@Head3 = Third level out-
line topic
```

When pretagging, special care must be taken to ensure correct spelling.

BodySetIn

Description and usage

Body text set in from left margin. Use BodySetIn for examples or long quotes.

BodySetIn helps define the hierarchy of the chapter by moving text in from the left margin as a block .

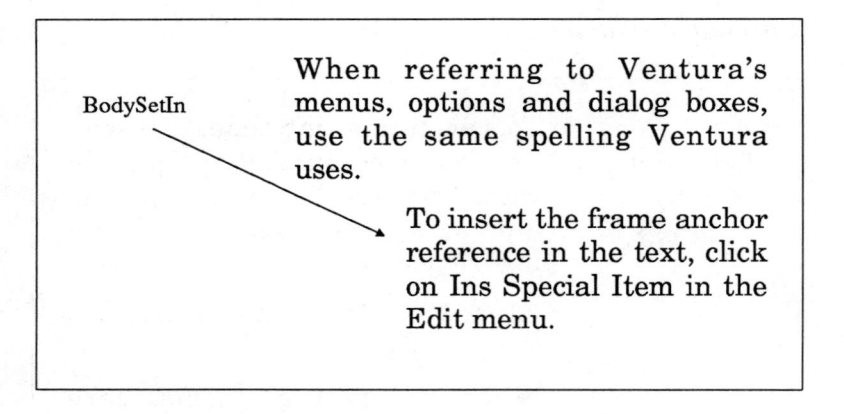

Formatted example

> BodySetIn
>
> When referring to Ventura's menus, options and dialog boxes, use the same spelling Ventura uses.
>
> To insert the frame anchor reference in the text, click on Ins Special Item in the Edit menu.

Captions

Z_Caption

Description and usage
Picture caption.

Z_Caption is a generated tag created by Ventura. Authors type suggested captions into the manuscript, without referencing picture location. At layout time, editors cut the captions and paste them into separate caption frames. Do not type in the figure number; Ventura generates it automatically.

Word processing example

```
@Z_Caption = Crop marks appear outside the
page area.
```

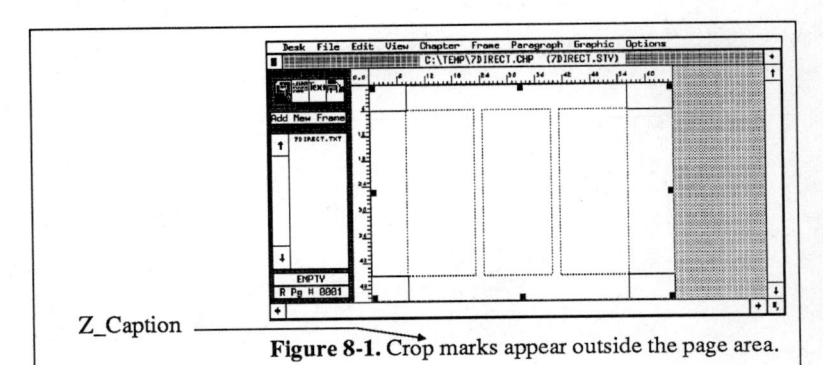

Formatted example

Z_Caption

Figure 8-1. Crop marks appear outside the page area.

Callouts

Z_Box Text

Description and usage
Generated tag for text positioned in graphics mode. Use for callouts — brief labels for parts of pictures.

Callouts are usually created in graphics mode. Lines are often used to connect them to pictures.

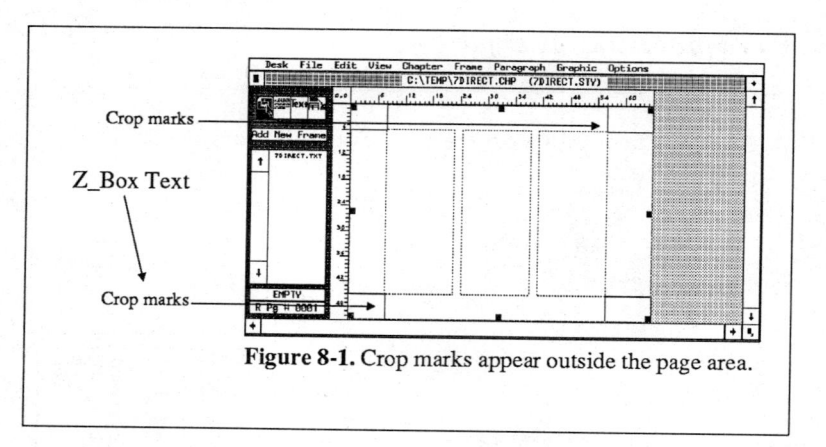

Formatted example

Figure 8-1. Crop marks appear outside the page area.

Headings and Titles

Head1

Description and usage
First-level heading. Use Head1 to highlight a main topic within a chapter.

Most chapters should have at least two (but not more than six) first-level headings. Headings signify chapter construction to readers and give continuity to the book. Make them brief but clear. Write all headings, including Head1, in down style (capitalize only the first word).

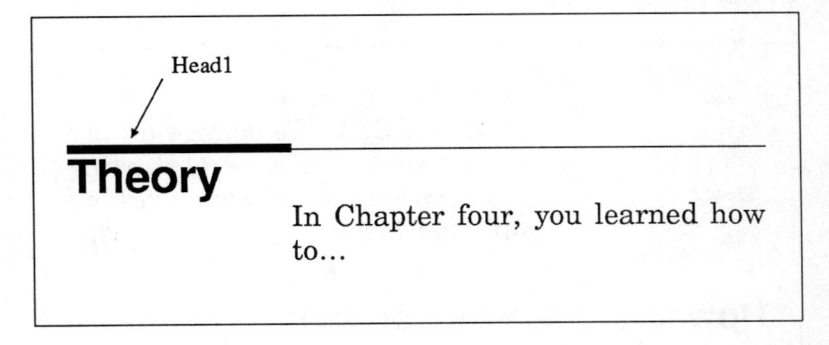

Formatted example

```
         Head1
          /
         ↓
    _____

    Theory
                In Chapter four, you learned how
                to...
```

Head2

Description and usage
Second-level heading. Use to break up main topics into subtopics.

Use similar sentence structure for all headings in the same level. For instance, if you begin your first Head2 with *How to*, consider starting them all that way. This gives the reader another clue about the book's information hierarchy. Use down style.

Formatted example

Head2 → Tags are controlled in the PARA-GRAPH MENU. To change a tag's attributes, we recommend starting at the top of this menu and working your way down.

How to choose font options

Font is the first menu option in the PARAGRAPH MENU. It controls Face, Size, Style and Color attributes of the paragraph, as well as limited spacing attributes (Shift and Kern).

Head 3

Description and usage
Third-level heading. Use to Head3 to break down subtopics into bite-size pieces.

Use third-level headings sparingly. It's not necessary to divide each subsection into sub-subsections. Use down style.

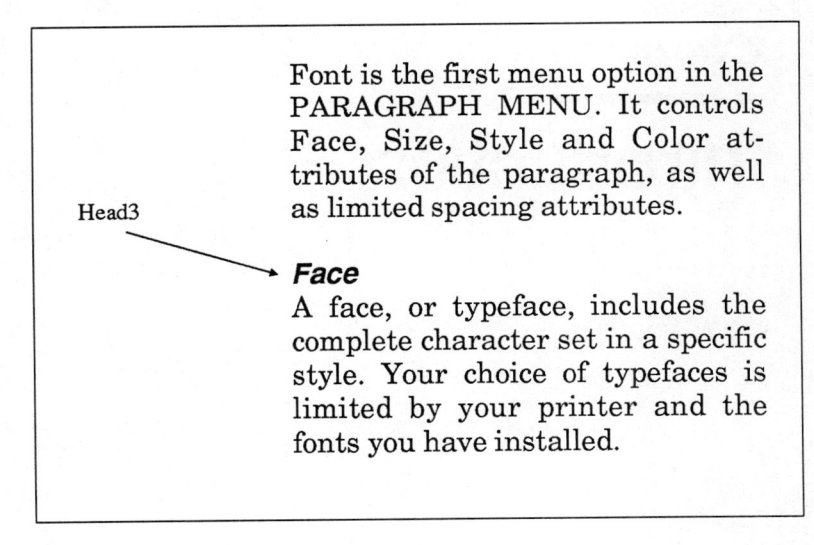

Formatted example

> Head3 → Font is the first menu option in the PARAGRAPH MENU. It controls Face, Size, Style and Color attributes of the paragraph, as well as limited spacing attributes.
>
> ### *Face*
> A face, or typeface, includes the complete character set in a specific style. Your choice of typefaces is limited by your printer and the fonts you have installed.

HeadChap

Description and Usage
The title of the chapter.

HeadChap or HeadChapNum is normally the largest of the head tags. HeadChap usually follows HeadChapNum.

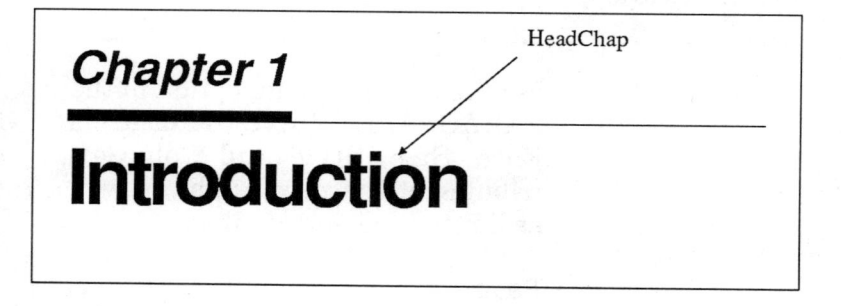

Formtted example

Chapter 1

Introduction ← HeadChap

HeadChapNum

Description and Usage
Chapter number.

HeadChapNum is usually the second element in each chapter (after DateMark), although it occasionally follows the title as well.

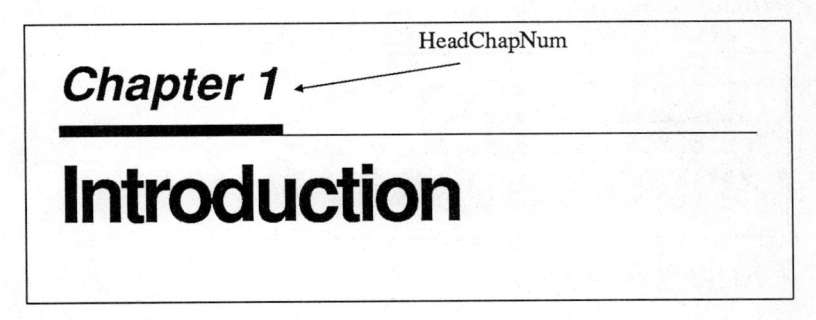

Formatted example

Chapter 1 ← HeadChapNum

Introduction

Lists

List2Col1

Description and usage

First column of a two-column version of ListBoxSolid, our instruction format. Use to give instructions in shorthand style.

Use List2Col1 with List2Col2 only to save space in documents. For most instructions to readers, use ListBoxSolid. Treat other two-column applications as tables.

Word processing example

```
To create the BodyCenter tag:
@List2Col1 = Alignment
@List2Col2 = Horz. Alignment: Center
@List2Col2 = Overall Width: Frame-Wide
```

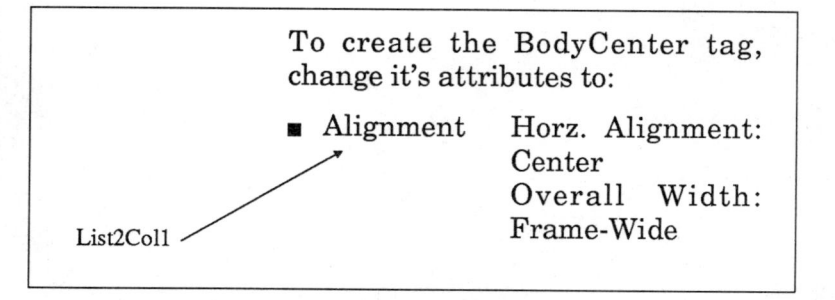

Formatted example

> To create the BodyCenter tag, change it's attributes to:
>
> ■ Alignment   Horz. Alignment: Center
>   Overall Width: Frame-Wide
>
> List2Col1

List2Col2

Description and usage
Second column of a two-column instruction format. Use to save space by giving instructions in "shorthand" styke,

Use List2Col2 *only* with List2Col1 for brief instructions. Treat all other two-column applications as tables.

Word processed example

```
To create the BodyCenter tag:
@List2Col1 = Alignment
@List2Col2 = Horz. Alignment: Center
@List2Col2 = Overall Width: Frame-Wide
```

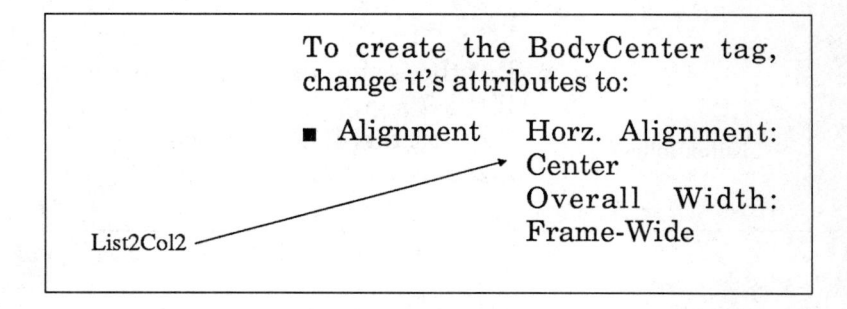

Formatted example

To create the BodyCenter tag, change it's attributes to:

■ Alignment   Horz. Alignment: Center
              Overall Width: Frame-Wide

List2Col2

ListBoxHollow

Description and usage
Bulleted list with square, hollow bullets.

We use ListBoxHollow for a summary of tips at the end of the chapter. You might also use it for checklists.

Formatted example

Pretagging Tips

□ Always use the format@TAG-NAME = . Make sure the tag name is the first thing in the paragraph.

□ Ventura assumes that any paragraph without a tag name is body text.

□ Put the @ sign in the left margin. If the @ sign is any other place in the text file, it will not be recognized as part of the tag code.

ListBoxHollow

ListBoxSolid

Description and usage
Bulleted list with square, solid bullets. Use ListBoxSolid for step-by-step instructions.

Use *only* for instructions. Any time readers see this square bullet, they should know they are expected to take an action.

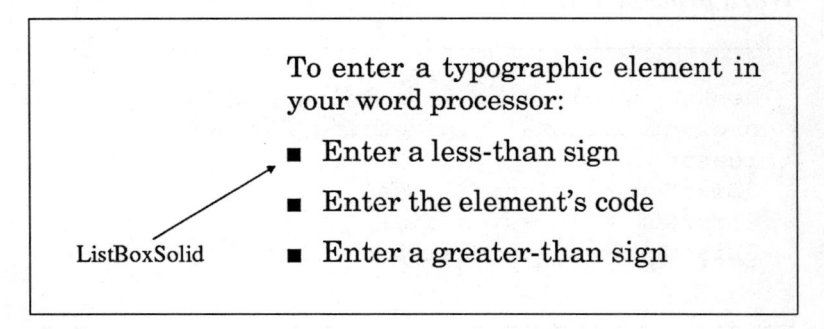

Formatted example

> To enter a typographic element in your word processor:
>
> - Enter a less-than sign
> - Enter the element's code
> - Enter a greater-than sign

(ListBoxSolid)

ListNum

Description and usage
Numbered list.

Use ListNum for a series which needs to be numbered.

Enter the list in your word processor *without* numbers, as shown. Ventura will insert the numbers automatically.

Word processed example

```
Desktop publishing is gaining popularity
over traditional typesetting for several
reasons:
@ListNum = It costs less.
@ListNum = It saves time.
@ListNum = It is easier to learn.
```

Formatted example

ListNumber

Desktop publishing is gaining popularity over traditional typesetting for several reasons:

1. It costs less.
2. It saves time.
3. It is easier to learn.

ListRound

Description and usage
Bulleted list with round bullets.

Bullets are recommended for lists of three to seven items within the main text, where it is not necessary to number the list. Bullet characters originate in Ventura — you do not need to type them in.

Word processed example

```
Newcomers to the graphic arts need to
learn some basic terminology before trying
desktop publishing. Typographical terms
which may be new to the novice include:
@ListRound = picas and points
@ListRound = ems and ens
@ListRound = callouts and captions
```

Formatted example

ListRound

Newcomers to the graphic arts need to learn some basic terminology before trying desktop publishing. Typographical terms which may be new to the novice include:

- picas and points
- ems and ens
- callouts and captions

Notes

Note

Description and usage
Important information. Use Note to call attention to the paragraph.

Use this tag when skipping the paragraph might create confusion or problems for readers.

Word processed example

```
In this section, you'll learn how to for-
mat reverse (or reverse video) type.
@Note = NOTE:  If you do not have a
postscript printer, you may not be able to
print the attributes explained below.
Print capabilities page to find out.
```

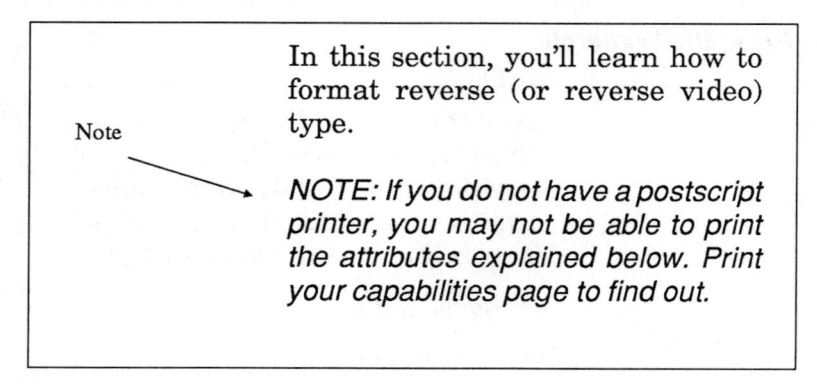

Formatted example

> In this section, you'll learn how to format reverse (or reverse video) type.
>
> Note →
>
> *NOTE: If you do not have a postscript printer, you may not be able to print the attributes explained below. Print your capabilities page to find out.*

NoteWarn

Description and usage
Critical information. Use NoteWarn to call attention to potentially dangerous conditions.

NoteWarn makes a stronger statement to readers than Note. Use it when skipping the paragraph might cause serious damage.

Formatted example

NoteWarn →

Once a newsletter design is completed, make a template. Include the headline, masthead, dateline, regular feature heads, etc. — everything but the articles. Each time you produce a new issue, open this template and save it as a new chapter.

WARNING: Save the template as a new chapter immediately to avoid the risk of overwriting and losing it.

Other

PictureMark

Description and usage
Picture location marker. Use PictureMark to tag the picture's filename at its location in the text file.

Enter the PictureMark tag, followed by the picture's file name, on a separate line whereyou want the picture to appear. (You can choose the file name as you write, before you actually create the picture.)

Word processing example

```
Crop marks print outside the page area to
indicate page size and cutting lines.

@PictureMark = MDAACROP.IMG
```

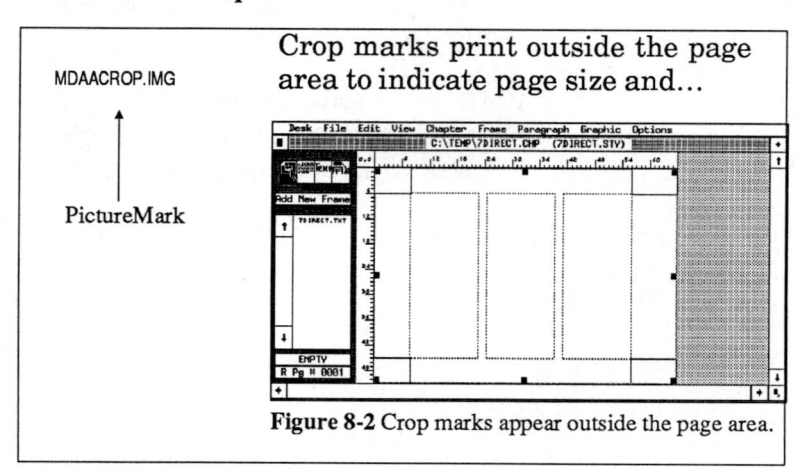

Formatted example

Figure 8-2 Crop marks appear outside the page area.

Tables

TableHead

Description and usage
Title of a table.

TableHead must be placed *before* Z_Tbl_Beg in the text file, or Ventura will refuse to format the table. Do not pretag any text between Z_Tbl_Beg and Z_Tbl_End.

Formatted example

Table A-1: Commonly used typographic characters available through bracket codes

Character	Symbol	Code
open quote	"	<169>
close quote	"	<170>
em dash	—	<197>
en dash	–	<196>
ellipsis	…	<193>

Z_Tbl_Beg

Description and usage
Beginning of a table. Use Z_Tbl_Beg to tell Ventura to start a table.

The paragraph should be empty except for the number of columns you want. The Z_Tbl_Beg tag is invisible in Ventura.

Word processed example

```
@Z_Tbl_Beg = COLUMNS(3)
```

Formatted example

Z_Tbl_Beg

Table A-2: Commonly used typographic characters available through bracket codes

Character	Symbol	Code
open quote	"	<169>
close quote	"	<170>
em dash	—	<197>
en dash	–	<196>
ellipsis	...	<193>

Z_Tbl_End

Description and usage

End of table. Use Z_Tbl_End to tell Ventura to end a table.

Assign Z_Tbl_End to an empty paragraph immediately following the table. The Z_Tbl_End tag is invisible in Ventura.

Word processing example

```
@Z_Tbl_End =
```

Formatted example

Table A-1: Commonly used typographic characters available through bracket codes

Character	Symbol	Code
open quote	"	<169>
close quote	"	<170>
em dash	—	<197>
en dash	–	<196>
ellipsis	...	<193>

← Z_Tbl_End

Sample Checklists 9

This chapter presents sample checklists for book, magazine, and newsletter production. The book checklists are very similar to the ones we use at New Riders.

Checklists serve the dual purpose of keeping everyone on track and making sure nothing gets left out of the publishing process. We create them as soon as we decide to go ahead with a project, and update them at least weekly. Checklists also serve as a centralized point for logging important publication data, such as Library of Congress information and page counts.

Magazine and newsletters share many facets of the production process, so we have grouped them into a single set of checklists. Line items that are usually applicable only to magazines have been indicated with an asterisk (*).

Use these checklists like all the other samples in this book: Modify them to fit your organization's needs. For your convenience, we have included text files and Ventura chapter and style files for these checklists on the optional disk.

Book production

The Manuscript Checklist lists every section in the book.

Manuscript Checklist

Title: _____

Description	1st Draft	2nd draft	Illustrations	First Layout	Final Layout
Title page					
Verso					
Author bio					
Production					
Disclaimer					
Dedication					
Acknowledgements					
Trademarks					
Table of Contents					
Introduction					
Chapters/Titles/Final page count					
Appendix					
Colophon					
Index					
Advertisement					
Order form					
Comment card					
Disk(s)					
Page count					

Checklists

The Production Checklist covers all the necessary steps in producing a book, from planning to archiving.

Production Checklist

Title: _____

Description	Responsible	Date Due	Date Done
Proforma Profit and Loss			
Sales questionnaire			
Set up paper files/checklists			
Letter of intent to author			
Contract			
Contract advance $ _____			
Style guide/tag list to author			
Review cover design and copy			
Begin manuscript (see checklist)			
Begin disk			
First draft/progress payment $ _____			
Second draft/progress payment $ _____			
Third draft/progress payment $ _____			
Request Library of Congress CIP # _____			
Request permissions			
Illustrations complete			
Printing Bids			
Cover mechanical			
Disk testing			
Disk master			
Final draft/progress payment $ _____			
Disk label mechanical			
Camera-ready to printer _____			
Disk to duplicator _____			
Proof bluelines			
Press and bindery check			
Register copyright			
Archive			

The Marketing & Notification Checklist lists various avenues for generating sales, and notes organizations to notify of the book's release.

Marketing & Notification Checklist

Title: _____

Description	Responsible	Date Due	Date Done
Prepublication offer			
Key accounts			
Book clubs			
Sub-rights offered			
Premium sales			
Catalog houses			
Seasonal/Group Promos/NR Catalog			
Direct mail			
Audio/Software			
Specialty outlets			
Key chain stores			
Libraries			
Government/Armed Services			
Education			
Foreign			
Exhibits			
PI ads			
Notify:			
CIP			
Bowker			
Baker & Taylor			
H.W. Wilson			
Books in Print			
ABA Book Buyer's Handbook			
Dustbook			
Small Press Record of Business Books			
Computer Publishers and Pubs			
Library Corporation			
National Association of College Stores			
Publishers' Trade List Annual			
Contemporary Authors			
Publisher's Weekly spring and fall			
Directory of Directories			
Publishers' Marketing Association			

The Promotion Checklist ensures that no possible means of promoting your book is overlooked.

Promotion Checklist

Title: _____

Description	Responsible	Date Due	Date Done
Solicit testimonials			
Reviewer list			
Review slip			
Press release possibilities			
Announcement			
Publication			
Giveaway			
Current news tie-in			
Famous personality tie-in			
Coop with other companies			
Date or event tie-in			
Promotional tour release			
Author			
Contest			
Research findings			
Second printing			
Second edition			
Selection by association			
Subsidiary rights sale			
Sales figures			
Awards			
Fact sheet			
Synopsis			
Author bio			
Brochure/flyer/catalog copy			
Send key account review copies			
Send mass review mailing			
Review follow up			
Article campaign			
Radio campaign			
Speaking campaign			
Second release			
Review marketing and notification checklist			

Magazine production

The Issue Overview addresses key decisions which must be made prior to beginning magazine/newsletter production.

Issue Overview

Publication _____
Editor _____
Art Director _____
Publication date _____
Cover date _____
Volume Number _____
Size:
    Flat _____
    Folded _____
Pages _____
Color(s) _____
Theme _____
Cover story _____
Cover concept _____
Cover illustrator/designer/photographer _____
Checklists completed:
    Advertiser Checklist completed (date) _____
    Article Checklist completed (date) _____
    Page Checklist completed (date) _____
    Scheduling Checklist completed (date) _____

The Scheduling Checklist provides a single location to record pertinent due dates for a magazine/newsletter issue.

Scheduling Checklist

Description	Responsible	Date Due	Date Done
Create checklists			
Preliminary planning meeting			
Issue overview complete			
Final planning meeting			
Cover concept			
Cover art assigned			
Assign writers			
Contributor contracts			
Assign articles			
1st drafts complete			
Assign illustrations/photographs			
2nd drafts complete			
*Cover art to color separator			
Format			
Masthead revised			
Datelines revised			
Format advertisements			
Advertisements to proof			
Illustrations/photographs in			
3rd drafts complete			
Cover to printer			
Camera-ready ads in			
*4-color illustrations/photographs to separator			
Final copy to printer			
*Check bluelines			
*Press check (optional)			
Printing and binding			
Distribution			

*May not be applicable to newsletters

The Article Checklist is used as a planning tool before production gets underway. It is useful throughout production for keeping authors and editors on schedule.

Article Checklist

Title	Responsible	1st draft	Illustrations	2nd draft	3rd draft	Final
Standing columns:						
Features:						

Checklists

9–9

The Advertiser Checklist aids in page planning, and helps schedule workflow through the production department.

Advertiser Checklist

Advertiser	Size	Formatted in-house:			Provided camera ready:	Page #
		Mockup	Proof	Final	Date due in	

The Page Checklist is essential for layout operators, who have to plug multiple articles, illustrations and ads into the proper position on each page. It is also helpful for planning story lengths.

Page Checklist

Page	Responsible	Date Due	Date Done
Front cover			
Back cover			
Inside front			
Inside back			
Page #/Content			

Bibliography and Resources 10

These are the books we recommend to our authors and editors. We have also included associations, magazines, and newsletters that you might find helpful.

Books

Beach, Mark. *Editing Your Newsletter: A Guide to Writing, Design, and Production.* Third Edition. Coast to Coast Books. (2934 NE 16th Avenue, Portland, OR 97212.) *A highly readable handbook that motivates as well as teaches.*

Beach, Mark; Shepro, Steven; and Russon, Ken. *Getting It Printed.* Coast to Coast Books. (2934 NE 16th Avenue, Portland, OR 97212.) *My favorite book on the process of putting words and pictures on paper. Helpful whether you're experienced or just beginning. This volume explains key topics in simple language, but also includes tips for advanced users.*

Canfield, Byron and Canty, Chad. *Style Sheets for Technical Documents.* New Riders Publishing. (P.O. Box 4846-V, Thousand Oaks, CA 91360.) Book and disk set. *Over 25 ready-to-use style sheets for Xerox Ventura Publisher, designed by seasoned professionals. Use them as is, modify them to suit your tastes, or simply adapt their advanced techniques to your own style sheets. Sophisticated enough to handle the most complex technical documents.*

Cavuoto, James and Berst, Jesse. *Inside Xerox Ventura Publisher, 2nd Edition.* New Riders Publishing. (P.O. Box 4846-V, Thousand Oaks, CA 91360.) Optional disk. *Whether you're a beginner or an old hand, all the information you need to produce professional documents with Ventura is presented in this volume. Covers Ventura Publisher Version 2.0 and Professional Extension.*

The Chicago Manual of Style. University of Chicago Press. (5801 South Ellis Avenue, Chicago, IL 60637.) *The style guide we fall back on when we do not already have an in-house rule to cover the situation. A huge, expensive, and overblown reference work, but worthwhile if you plan to make writing/editing your career.*

Flesch, Rudolf. *The Art of Readable Writing.* Macmillan Publishing Co., Inc. (866 Third Avenue, New York, NY 10022.) *The first book to espouse writing principles based on readability research. Still one of the best. Will help you learn to trim the fat.*

Gunning, Robert. *The Technique of Clear Writing.* McGraw Hill, Inc. (1221 Avenue of the Americas, New York, NY 10020.) *A challenging and helpful book which includes ten easy-to-follow guidelines for clear, readable writing. Although originally published as a scholarly effort, Gunning's friendly tone keeps this book surprisingly engaging and contemporary.*

Judd, Karen. *Copyediting: A Practical Guide.* William Kaufmann, Inc. (95 First Street, Los Altos, CA 94022.) *If you want to learn copyediting, this is the book. It covers not only the rules of grammar and usage, but also the mechanics of copyediting. Although slanted towards traditional methods, most of the tools and tips can be adapted to electronic editing.*

Lubow, Martha and Berst, Jesse. *Publishing Power with Ventura.* New Riders Publishing. (P.O. Box 4846-V, Thousand Oaks, CA 91360.) Optional disk. *Learn the ins and outs of Ventura Publisher Version 2 by creating actual documents with this hands-on tutorial. Perfect for training and self-paced learning.*

Lubow, Martha and Berst, Jesse. *Style Sheets for Business Documents*. New Riders Publishing. (P.O. Box 4846-V, Thousand Oaks, CA 91360.) Book and disk set. *Over 30 business style sheets developed by professionals. Ready to accept your text for instant, effective documents. Includes style sheets for everything from letters to brochures, plus over 10 0 pages of design tips and techniques.*

Lubow, Martha and Pattison, Polly. *Style Sheets for Newsletters*. New Riders Publishing. (P.O. Box 4846-V, Thousand Oaks, CA 91360.) Book and disk set. *A library of over 26 newsletter templates created by graphic designers. Just load text and print. Style sheets range from simple to complex, in one to five column formats. Also presents techniques for effective design.*

Nelson, Roy Paul. *Publication Design*. W.C. Brown Co. (2460 Kerper Boulevard, DuBuque, IA 52001.) *A scholarly but useful overall introduction to design for all kinds of publications.*

Pocket Pal. International Paper Co. (220 East 42nd Street, New York, NY 10017.) *Considered the classic reference for anyone involved in print production. I've never felt it lives up to its reputation — it's too cryptic. Nevertheless, I must admit that it's handy and quick. There are many who swear by it.*

Price, Jonathan. *How to Write a Computer Manual*. The Benjamin/Cummings Publishing Co. (2727 Sand Hill Road, Menlo Park, CA 94025.) *Of the books on how to write about computers, this is our favorite. By a former Apple employee and one of the people who pioneered the idea of reader-friendly documentation. Covers organization, planning, research, writing, editing, usage, style, and more.*

Strunk, William Jr., and White, E. B. *Elements of Style*. Macmillan Publishing Co., Inc. (866 Third Avenue, New York, NY 10022.) *The all-time classic. Takes an hour or two to read cover to cover. Worth every minute despite its slightly archaic tone and language. Covers both usage and style.*

White, Jan. *Editing by Design.* R.R. Bowker. (Distributed by Dynamic Graphics Bookshelf, Box 1901, Peoria, IL 61614.) *A classic by one of the acknowledged gurus of American graphic design.*

White, Jan. *Graphic Design for the Electronic Age: The manual for traditional and desktop publishing.* Watson-Guptill. (1515 Broadway, New York, NY 10036.) *A thorough and up-to-date espousal of White's design philosophy, adapted for use with today's publishing technologies.*

Xerox Corp. *Xerox Publishing Standards.* Watson-Gustill Publications. (1515 Broadway, New York, NY 10036.) *A few years back, Xerox set out to develop an in-house guide for writing and design. The result is this 400-page, 8.5x11 in. tome, which is now available to the public. Although you may not agree with all the conclusions, you are sure to find many interesting ideas and helpful techniques. A useful example of an in-house style guide taken to the extreme.*

Magazines & Newsletters

EP&P. 29 N. Wacker Drive, Chicago, IL 60606. (312) 726-2802 (inside IL) (800) 621-9907 (outside IL).

MicroPublishing Report. 21150 Hawthorne Blvd. #104, Torrance, CA 90503. (213) 371-5787.

Personal Publishing. 25W550 Geneva Road, Wheaton, IL 60188-2292. (312) 665-1000 (inside IL), (800) 627-7201 (outside IL).

Publish!. 501 Second Street, San Francisco, CA 94107. (303) 447-9330 (inside CO), (800) 525-0643 (outside CO).

Associations

International Association of Business Communicators. One Hallidie Plaza, Suite 600, San Francisco, CA 94102. (415) 433-3400.

National Association of Desktop Publishers. PO Box 508, Kenmore Station, Boston, MA 02215-9998. (617) 437-6472.

Ventura Publisher Users' Group. 7502 Aaron Place, San Jose, CA 95139. (408) 227-5030. *The national umbrella organization for Ventura users, which can direct you to a local chapter. Services include a monthly magazine and an on-line bulletin board.*

Society for Technical Communication. Department 5045, Washington, DC 20061-5405. (202) 737-0035. *This international organization can direct you to local chapters in 42 states and five countries. Membership benefits include a quarterly journal and monthly newsletter.*

Installing the Optional Disk

Appendix A

The optional Managing disk contains text files, style sheets, and chapter files that duplicate three chapters from the book:
- Chapter Six, "Sample Grammar and Usage Guide"
- Chapter Seven, "Sample Writing Guide"
- Chapter Eight, "Tag Dictionary"

In addition, it contains the production checklists shown in Chapter Nine, "Sample Checklists."

The Managing disk can save time and effort in several ways. The idea is to use its samples as the starting point for documents of your own. You may be able to save yourself hours of typing by customizing the examples rather than starting from scratch.

If you work with Xerox Ventura Publisher, you can also save formatting time. The disk includes everything you need to load and print all four chapters with Ventura. Or, if you like the format but wish to substitute text of your own, you can use the style sheet by itself. Chapters Six, Seven, and Eight are compatible with Ventura Version 2. Chapter Nine requires Version 2 with the Professional Extension. Although Chapter Nine will print out in Version 2, it will not be properly formatted without the table mode available only in the Professional Extension.

Even if you do not use Xerox Ventura Publisher, you can still load the text files into the word processor or page-layout program of your choice. They are in ASCII format.

Backing up the disk

Before starting, make a copy of the disk using the DOS command DISKCOPY or the DOS function COPY. Store the original in a safe place and use the copy as the working disk.

The Managing disk is copyrighted. It is intended for your personal use. It may not be sold or transferred for profit.

Contents of the disk

Table A-1: Files on the optional Managing disk

Category	File name	Brief description
Miscellaneous	HELP.BAT	Batch file for displaying README.1ST on screen
	MANAGE.PUB	Ventura publication for copying all chapters at one time
	MDREADME.1ST	Disk instructions
	MDUPDATE.TXT	Information about last-minute changes and corrections (if any)
Chapter Six, "Sample Grammar and Usage Guide"	MD06.CHP	Chapter file
	MD06.CIF	Information file
	MD.STY	Style sheet
	MD06.VGR	Graphics file
	MD06.CAP	Caption file
	MD06.TXT	ASCII text file

Appendix A   A – 3

Category	File name	Brief description
Chapter Seven, "Sample Writing Guide"	MD07.CHP	Chapter file
	MD07.CIF	Information file
	MD.STY	Style sheet
	MD07.VGR	Graphics file
	MD07.CAP	Caption file
	MD07TRAN.TXT	ASCII text file
	MD07.TXT	ASCII text file
Chapter Eight, "Tag Dictionary"	MD08.CHP	Chapter file
	MD08.CIF	Information file
	MD.STY	Style sheet
	MD08.VGR	Graphics file
	MD08.CAP	Caption file
	MD08CRPA.IMG	Image file
	MD08SCRN.IMG	Image file
	MD08SMP1.EPS	Postscript picture file
	MD08SMP2.EPS	Postscript picture file
	MD08.TXT	ASCII text file
Chapter Nine, "Sample Checklists"	MDCHKLST.CHP	Chapter file
	MDCHKLST.CIF	Information file
	MDCHKLST.STY	Style sheet
	MDCHKLST.CAP	Caption file
	MD09CHKB.TXT	ASCII text file
	MD09CHKM.TXT	ASCII text file

Scanning MDREADME.1ST

Begin by scanning the MDREADME.1ST file for changes or corrections:

- Turn on your system.
- When you see the DOS prompt, put the working disk in drive A:.
- change to the A: drive by typing:

- To stop the screen from scrolling, type Ctrl-S. Type Ctrl-S again to resume scrolling.
- For a printout of the file, turn on your printer and type:
  `COPY MDREADME.1ST PRN [Enter]`

Using the text files

To use the text files alone, copy them from the floppy disk to the disk and subdirectory of your choice. For instance, the following command will copy all the text files from the A: drive to the C:\SAMPLE subdirectory:
`COPY A:*.TXT C:\SAMPLE`

Substitute your actual destination drive and subdirectory in place of C:\SAMPLE.

Using the style sheets

To use either of the style sheets on their own, copy them from the floppy disk to the disk and subdirectory of your choice. For instance, the following command will copy both style sheets from the A: drive to the C:\SAMPLE subdirectory:
`COPY A:*.STY C:\SAMPLE`

Installing the disk with Ventura

If you wish to use the Ventura chapter files included on the disk, you must use Ventura's Multi-Chapter function to move them to the disk and subdirectory of your choice. If you use the DOS COPY function instead, they will not operate correctly. The following instructions explain how to copy the the files from the A: drive to the C:\SAMPLE subdirectory.

- Place the working disk in the A: drive and close the door.
- Load Xerox Ventura Publisher. Once it is on the screen, select Multi-Chapter from the Options menu. You do not need to open a chapter.
- If you see a chapter highlighted, deselect by clicking anywhere else inside the Multi-Chapter dialog box.

Appendix A A–5

- Select Open from the list at the side of the dialog box. The Item Selector appears.

- Move the cursor to the Directory line. Press Esc to clear the line and type:
  A:*.PUB

Ventura looks on the A: drive for publications. An Item Selector appears. It shows only one publication, called MANAGE.PUB.

- Click on MANAGE.PUB to select it. Click OK.

- The Multi-Chapter dialog box now shows a list of the chapters that make up the publication.

- Select Copy All from the list at the right side of the dialog box.

- The Copy All dialog box appears. At the top is a Source section. Confirm that it shows the publication A:\MANAGE.PUB.

- Move the cursor to the line labeled PUB & CHPS. Press Esc to clear the line. Type in the name of your destination subdirectory:
  C:\SAMPLE

- Click once on the button titled Make All Directories the Same As the First.

- Confirm that all the lines now read C:\SAMPLE and click OK.

Ventura begins copying files. During the process, the following message will appear:
```
This file could not be found: A:\OUTPUT.WID.
Do you wish to skip over it or retry with a
new disk, or cancel the archive process?
```

- Choose Skip (the uppermost button).

When Ventura has finished copying, it returns you to the Multi-Chapter dialog box.

- Click on Done.

- Remove the Manage disk from the A: drive. You are ready to begin.

Disclaimer

The Managing disk is subject to change at any time without notice. It is provided on an as-is basis, as a convenience. New Riders Publishing is not liable or responsible to any person or entity with respect to any loss or damage in connection with or arising from the use of the disk.

Index

A

Abbreviations 6-4
    keys 6-14
Acronyms 6-4, 6-6
Active voice 7-20
Affect 6-4
Although 6-4
Antecedents 7-19
Apostrophes 6-5
Appendixes
    naming files 2-6
Archiving 2-13, 5-16
Art log 5-12
Authors
    approving editing changes 4-4
    tool kit 1-13, 2-33
AutoCAD 3-5

B

Backup
    See Archiving
Boldface
    for emphasis 6-5

Books
    production checklist 9-2
Bracket codes
    table of common codes 2-18
Bullet lists 6-16

C

Can, may 6-5
Capitalization
    chapter numbers 6-6
    computer acronyms 6-6
    dialog boxes 6-6
    file names 6-7
    headings 6-7
    hyphenated compounds 6-7
    initial caps 6-6
    lower case 6-6
    menus 6-7
    notes 6-7
    parts of the book 6-7
    terminology 6-5
    upper and lower 6-6
Captions 3-21, 6-8
Checklists
    copyediting 4-11, 4-13

production 9-1
proofreading 4-17
Colons 6-8
Commas 6-9
Comparisons 7-31
Consistency 7-27
Contractions 6-10
Conversational style 7-29
Converting files 4-6
Copyediting
   checklists 4-11
   definition 4-6
   grammar guide 4-8
   spelling glossary 4-9
   style list 4-10
   writing guide 4-8
Corrections
   when editing 4-3, 4-5

D

DateMark tag 2-24
Dating files 2-24
Disk labels 5-14
Disk, optional A-1
Drawing programs 3-5

E

E.g. 6-10
Editing
   author approval 4-4
   copyediting 4-6
   developmental 4-6
   entering corrections 4-3, 4-5
   major issues 4-5

mechanics 4-2
paper vs. screen 4-2
proofreading 4-15
redlining 4-4
revisions 4-5
tool kit 1-14, 4-24
working with others 4-4
WP vs. DTP 4-3
Effect 6-4
Ellipses 6-10
Em dash 6-11
En dash 6-12
Encapsulated PostScript
   See EPS files
Ensure 6-12
EPS files 3-7
Examples 7-31
Exclamation marks 6-12
Extensions
   text files 2-8

F

Files
   archiving 2-13, 5-16
   capitalization of names 6-7, 6-12
   conversion 2-14, 4-6, 5-3
   dating 2-24
   dividing material 2-2
   extensions 2-8, 3-17
   locating 2-11
   Macintosh names 2-3
   MS-DOS names 2-3
   naming 2-2, 2-9
   organizing 1-4, 2-1
   picture 5-5
   preformatting 2-14, 2-16

text 2-13
text files 2-2, 2-9
transferring to other systems 2-3
Unix names 2-3
Filing
    paper files 5-2
    standard system 5-2
Five phases of DTP 1-7
Folders
    See Subdirectories
Footers 2-23
Footnotes 2-23
Formatting
    checklists 5-13
    copyediting checklists 4-15
    documenting 5-7
    file conversion 5-3
    headers and footers 2-23
    hyphenation 2-23
    indents 2-20
    job tracking 5-14
    lists 2-21
    organizing 5-2
    page layout 5-5
    pictures 3-2
    preformatting 2-14, 2-25, 5-5
    proofreading checklist 4-17
    standards 5-6
    tables 2-20, 3-8
    tabs vs. spaces 2-20
    tag dictionaries 2-30, 5-8
    tag lists 2-28
    tips and techniques 5-13
    tool kit 1-15, 5-17
Fractions 6-17
    See Numbers
Front matter
    naming files 2-6

G

Glossary, Spelling 4-9
Grammar
    copyediting checklists 4-14
    guide 4-8, 6-2
    importance 6-3

H

Hard disk organization
    See Subdirectories
Headers 2-23
Headings 7-13
    capitalization 6-7
HotShot
    See Screen captures
Humor 7-32
Hyphenation 2-23
Hyphens 6-11

I

I.e. 6-13
Illustrators
    tool kit 1-14, 3-24
Improving tone 7-29
In order to 6-13
Inches 6-18
Indexing 4-20
    "see also" entries 4-23
    "see" entries 4-23
    in text file 2-23
    main entries 4-22
    secondary entries 4-22
    what to include 4-22

Input 6-13
Installing the Managing disk A-1
Insure 6-13
Introductions 7-10
Italics 6-13

J

Job tracking 1-10, 5-14

K

Keylines 3-9
Keys 6-14

L

Layout
   See Page Layout
Like vs. such as 6-15
Lists 2-21
   bullet 6-16
   different types 6-16
   usage rules 6-16

M

Magazines
   production checklists 9-6
Managing disk A-1
Manuscripts
   indexing 4-20
Measurements
   See numbers
Money 6-18

N

Naming files 2-2, 2-9
   appendixes 2-6
   chapter codes 2-4
   file extensions 2-4
   front matter 2-6
   general rules 2-4
   pictures 3-13
   special sections 2-6
   table of contents 2-6
   text files 2-2, 2-9
Naming subdirectories 2-12
Newsletters
   production checklists 9-6
Non-keyboard characters
   See Special characters
Numbers
   dimensions 6-17
   fractions 6-17
   inches 6-18
   money 6-18
   nine or less 6-17
   page sizes 6-18
   percentages 6-18
   plurals 6-18
   ten or greater 6-17
   Ventura numbers 6-19

O

Organizing
   a project 1-3, 1-7, 5-2

files 2-1
people 1-5
subdirectories 2-12
testing organization 7-16
the office 1-4
writing 7-3
Outlining 7-3
Output 6-19

P

Page design
    documenting 5-7
    tag dictionaries 5-8
Page layout 5-5
    assigning responsibilities 4-6
    checklists 5-13
    converting files 4-6
    organizing 5-2
    pictures 3-2
    preformatting 5-5
Page sizes 6-18
Paragraphs 7-24
    topic sentences 7-24
    transitions 7-24
Parentheses 6-19
Parenthetical expressions
    usage rules 6-19
Passive voice 7-20
Percentages 6-18
Periods 6-20
Photos 3-9
PictureMark tag 3-18
Pictures
    art log 5-12
    callouts 3-22
    captions 3-21, 6-8

creating 3-2
drawing programs 3-4 to 3-5
electronic art 3-3
EPS files 3-7
file conversion 5-5
file extensions 3-17
general rules 3-3
keylines 3-9
locating 3-17
marking in text file 3-18
methods of creating 3-3
naming files 3-13
photos 3-9
PictureMark tag 3-18
printout 3-13
proofreading 4-20
scanned art 3-8
screen captures 3-7
standard sizes 3-11
templates 3-12
text references 2-21, 5-11
thumbnail sketches 3-4
tips and techniques 5-11
Point of view 7-30
Preformatting 2-14, 2-25, 5-5
    for Ventura 2-15
    rules 2-16
    tag dictionaries 2-30
    tag lists 2-28
    text files 2-25
Present tense 7-22
Project management
    See Job tracking
Proofreading
    checklists 4-17
    definition 4-15
    marks 4-17
    pictures 4-20

tables 4-19
tips 4-16
Punctuation
   colons 6-8
   commas 6-9
   ellipses 6-10
   em dash 6-11
   en dash 6-12
   exclamation marks 6-12
   hyphens 6-11 to 6-12
   parentheses 6-19
   periods 6-20
   question marks 6-20
   quotation marks 6-21
   semicolons 6-21

Q

Question marks 6-20
Quotation marks 6-21

R

Redlining 4-4
Revisions 5-16
   when editing 4-5

S

Scanned art 3-8
Screen captures 3-7
Second person 7-30
Semicolons 6-21
Sentences 7-20
   topic 7-24

   varying length 7-23
Special characters 2-17
Spelling
   glossary 4-9, 6-2
Standards
   formatting 5-6
   pictures 3-11
Style
   active vs. passive 7-20
   conversational 7-29
   examples and comparisons 7-31
   humor 7-32
   improving tone 7-29
   paragraphs 7-24
   point of view 7-30
   present tense 7-22
   second person 7-30
   sentence length 7-23
   sentences 7-20
   topic sentences 7-24
   transitions 7-24
   word choice 7-18
   wordiness 7-23
Style list 4-10
Style sheets 5-10
Subdirectories 2-11
   for pictures 3-17
   naming conventions 2-12
   See also Organizing
Summaries 7-16

T

Table of contents
   naming files 2-6
Tables 2-20
   as illustrations 3-8

formatting 3-8
proofreading 4-19
Tag dictionaries 2-30, 5-8, 8-1
Tag lists 2-28, 8-2
Tags
   DateMark 2-24
   naming 8-1
   PictureMark 3-18
Templates 5-8
   libraries 5-10
   pictures 3-12
Text
   attributes 2-17
   file extensions 2-8
   file naming 2-2, 2-9
   footnotes 2-23
   headers and footers 2-23
   hyphenation 2-23
   indents 2-20
   indexing 4-20
   lists 2-21
   preformatting 2-25, 5-5
   special characters 2-17
   tables 2-20
   tabs vs. spaces 2-20
   tag lists 2-28
   typing guidelines 2-13
   See also Files, Word processing
Text editing
   See Editing
Text files
   dating 2-24
   extensions 2-8
   naming 2-2, 2-9
   preformatting 2-25
   subdividing 2-2
   tables inside 2-2
Text references 2-21, 5-11

That 6-22
Thumbnail sketches 3-4
Tool kit
   creating 1-12
   for authors 1-13, 2-33
   for editors 1-14, 4-24
   for formatting 1-14, 5-17
   for illustrators 1-14, 3-24
Training 1-6
Transitions 7-24
Typographic characters
   See Special characters

U

Usage
   See Grammar

V

Verbs 6-22

W

Which
   See That
While 6-4
Word choice 7-18
Word processing
   file conversion 5-4
Wordiness 7-23
Writing
   active vs. passive 7-20
   applying structure 7-9
   consistency 7-27

examples and comparisons 7-31
grammar guide 6-2
guide 4-8
headings 7-13
humor 7-32
improving tone 7-29
introductions 7-10
organizing 7-3
paragraphs 7-24
present tense 7-22
second person 7-30
sentence length 7-23
sentences 7-20
summaries 7-16
topic sentences 7-24
transitions 7-24
verbs 6-22
word choice 7-18
wordiness 7-23

New Riders' Library

Bestselling how-to books, reference guides, learning materials, and companion disks for corporate and technical publishing from the desktop. Use the postage-paid card at the back of the book to order today.

INSIDE XEROX VENTURA PUBLISHER
James Cavuoto and Jesse Berst
704 pages, 330 illustrations
ISBN 0-934035-59-8 **$24.95**
2nd Edition

The best reference guide to Ventura Publisher is now even better! *Inside Xerox Ventura Publisher*, 2nd Edition, has been completely rewritten for Ventura Publisher Version 2 and includes more of what readers have asked for: more hands-on examples, more easy-to-use charts, and more time-saving tips and tricks.

PUBLISHING POWER WITH VENTURA
The Complete Teaching Guide to Xerox Ventura Publisher
Martha Lubow and Jesse Berst
704 pages, 230 illustrations
ISBN 0-934035-61-X **$27.95**
2nd Edition

Unlock the inner secrets of Ventura Publisher Version 2 with this well-written tutorial. You'll learn how to create your own great-looking business documents by producing the "real world" documents presented in this book. These documents include reports, newsletters, directories, technical manuals, and books. Companion software is available.

New Riders' Library

DESKTOP MANAGER
(Software)
ISBN: 0-934035-34-2 $99.95
Supports Version 1 and 2

Desktop Manager is the desktop accessory software for IBM and compatible personal computers that helps your manage your Ventura Publisher documents, running transparently from within the Ventura Publisher environment. A multifunction software utility, *Desktop Manager* provides file management, timed backup, document control, style sheet settings, and report generation. This essential utility program comes complete with an 180-page guide.

STYLE SHEETS FOR BUSINESS DOCUMENTS
(Book and Disk Set)
Martha Lubow and Jesse Berst
320 pages, 150 illustrations
ISBN 0-934035-22-9 $39.95
Supports Version 1 and 2

Introducing a cure for the common document—*Style Sheets for Business Documents*. This book and disk set contains more than 30 predesigned Ventura Publisher templates for creating top-quality business documents. Style sheets are presented for proposals, reports, marketing materials, ads, brochures, and correspondence. More than 100 pages of design tips and tricks are also included.

STYLE SHEETS FOR TECHNICAL DOCUMENTS
(Book and Disk Set)
By Byron Canfield and Chad Canty
320 Pages 150 illustrations
ISBN: 0-934035-29-6 $39.95
Supports Version 1 and 2

Get the maximum out of Ventura Publisher with these advanced technical document formats. This book/disk combination presents more than 25 ready-to-use templates for creating technical documents and books. Also includes techniques for creating pictures and tables, plus advanced tips for modifying formats to fit your needs.

STYLE SHEETS FOR NEWSLETTERS
(Book and Disk Set)
By Martha Lubow and Polly Pattison
320 Pages over 150 illustrations
ISBN: 0-934035-31-8 **$39.95**
Supports Version 1 and 2

This book and disk set presents more than 25 predesigned Ventura Publisher templates for creating one-, two-, three-, and four-column newsletters. Just open the chapter template, load in your own text, and print. A complete description of every style sheet and key tag for all chapter templates is also included.

MANAGING DESKTOP PUBLISHING
By Jesse Berst
320 Pages over 150 illustrations
ISBN: 0-934035-27-X **$9.95**

The essential handbook for the modern writer and editor. *Managing Desktop Publishing* shows you how to save production time by preformatting documents. Learn to manage your files, styles and style sheets. Also presented are the elements of style you need to succeed in today's desktop publishing arena. Companion software is available.

New Riders Library includes books on AutoCAD

INSIDE AUTOCAD   *Release 10*
D. Raker and H. Rice
750 pages, over 400 illustrations
ISBN: 0-934035-49-0 **$29.95**

INSIDE AutoCAD, the best selling book on AutoCAD, is entirely new and rewritten for AutoCAD's 3D Release 10. This easy-to-understand book serves as both a tutorial and a lasting reference guide.

New Riders' Library

### INSIDE AUTOLISP	Release 10
J. Smith and R. Gesner
672 pages, over 150 illustrations
ISBN: 0-934035-47-4 **$29.95**

Introducing the most comprehensive book on AutoLISP for AutoCAD Release 10. Learn AutoLISP commands and functions and write your own custom AutoLISP programs.

INSIDE AUTOSKETCH
By Frank Lenk
240 pages, over 120 illustrations
ISBN: 0-934035-20-2 **$17.95**

INSIDE AutoSketch gives you real-life mechanical parts, drawing schematics, and architectural drawings.

### CUSTOMIZING AUTOCAD	Release 10
J. Smith and R. Gesner
480 pages, over 100 illustrations
ISBN: 0-934035-45-8 **$27.95**

Uncover the hidden secrets of AutoCAD's 3D Release 10 in this all new edition. Discover the anatomy of an AutoCAD menu and build a custom menu from start to finish.

AUTOCAD FOR ARCHITECTS AND ENGINEERS
Release 10
John Albright and Elizabeth Schaeffer
480 pages, over 160 illustrations
ISBN: 0-934035-53-9 **$29.95**

Learn by doing a typical AEC project using high-powered design development with AutoCAD Release 10. Learn to construct working drawings using techniques from real life AEC projects.

### STEPPING INTO AUTOCAD	Release 10
By Mark Merickel
380 pages, over 140 illustrations
ISBN: 0-934035-51-2 **$29.95**

This popular tutorial has been completely rewritten with new exercises for Release 10. The book is organized to lead you step by step from the basics to practical tips on customizing AutoCAD for technical drafting.

AUTOCAD REFERENCE GUIDE   Release 10
By Dorothy Kent
256 pages, over 50 illustrations
ISBN: 0-934035-57-1   **$11.95**

All essential AutoCAD functions and commands are arranged alphabetically and described in just a few paragraphs.

THE AUTODESK FILE
Written and Edited by John Walker
608 pages
ISBN 0-934035-63-6   **$24.95**

The unvarnished history of Autodesk, Inc., the company behind AutoCAD. Read the original memos, letters and reports that trace the rise of Autodesk, from start-up to their present position as the number one CAD software company in the world.

Order from New Riders Publishing Today

Name: _____

Company: _____

Address: _____

City: _____

State: _____ Zip: _____

Phone: _____

The easiest way to order is to pick-up the phone and call **(818) 991-5392** between 9:00 AM and 5:00 PM PST. Please have your credit card available and your order can be placed in a snap!

Please indicate Version of Xerox Ventura you use.
- ☐ **Version 1.1** ☐ **Version 2**

Yes, please send me the productivity-boosting material I have checked below. Make check payable to New Riders Publishing.
- ☐ Check enclosed.
- ☐ Charge to my credit card:
- ☐ **Visa #** _____
- ☐ **Mastercard #** _____

Expiration date: _____ Signature: _____

Quantity	Description of Item	Unit Cost	Total Cost
	Managing Desktop Publishing	$ 9.95	
	Managing Desktop Publishing Disk	$ 7.95	
	Inside Xerox Ventura Publisher 2nd Edition	$24.95	
	Publishing Power with Ventura 2nd Edition	$27.95	
	Publishing Power Disk	$14.95	
	Style Sheets for Business Documents—Book/Disk Set	$39.95	
	Style Sheets for Newsletters—Book/Disk Set	$39.95	
	Style Sheets for Technical Documents—Book/Disk Set	$39.95	
	Desktop Manager (Software)	$99.95	
	All three Style Sheets (*Value Pack Save $19.90*)	$99.95	
MDP	Shipping and Handling: see information below.		
	Sales Tax: Californians please add 6.5% sales tax.		
	Total Amount		

Shipping and Handling: $4.00 for the first book and $1.75 for each additional book. Floppy disk: add $1.75 for shipping and handling. If you have to have it NOW, we can ship product to you in 24 to 48 hours for an additional charge and you will receive your item over night or in 2 days.

New Riders Publishing • P.O. Box 4846 • Thousand Oaks, CA 91360 • Phone: 818-991-5392 FAX: 818-991-9263

BUSINESS REPLY MAIL
FIRST CLASS   PERMIT NO. 53   THOUSAND OAKS, CA

POSTAGE WILL BE PAID BY ADDRESSEE

New Riders Publishing
P.O. Box 4846
Thousand Oaks, CA 91359-9968

NO POSTAGE
NECESSARY
IF MAILED
IN THE
UNITED STATES

Order from New Riders Publishing Today

Name: _____

Company: _____

Address: _____

City: _____

State: _____ Zip: _____

Phone: _____

The easiest way to order is to pick-up the phone and call **(818) 991-5392** between 9:00 AM and 5:00 PM PST. Please have your credit card available and your order can be placed in a snap!

Please indicate Version of Xerox Ventura you use.
- ☐ **Version 1.1**   ☐ **Version 2**

Yes, please send me the productivity-boosting material I have checked below. Make check payable to New Riders Publishing.
- ☐ Check enclosed.
- ☐ Charge to my credit card:
- ☐ Visa # _____
- ☐ Mastercard # _____

Expiration date: _____

Signature: _____

Quantity	Description of Item	Unit Cost	Total Cost
	Managing Desktop Publishing	$ 9.95	
	Managing Desktop Publishing Disk	$ 7.95	
	Inside Xerox Ventura Publisher 2nd Edition	$24.95	
	Publishing Power with Ventura 2nd Edition	$27.95	
	Publishing Power Disk	$14.95	
	Style Sheets for Business Documents–Book/Disk Set	$39.95	
	Style Sheets for Newsletters–Book/Disk Set	$39.95	
	Style Sheets for Technical Documents–Book/Disk Set	$39.95	
	Desktop Manager (Software)	$99.95	
	All three Style Sheets (*Value Pack Save $19.90*)	$99.95	
	Shipping and Handling: see information below.		
	Sales Tax: Californians please add 6.5% sales tax.		
MDP	**Total Amount**		

Shipping and Handling: $4.00 for the first book and $1.75 for each additional book. Floppy disk: add $1.75 for shipping and handling. If you have to have it NOW, we can ship product to you in 24 to 48 hours for an additional charge and you will receive your item over night or in 2 days.

New Riders Publishing ● P.O. Box 4846 ● Thousand Oaks, CA 91360 ● Phone: 818-991-5392   FAX: 818-991-9263